Democracy and the Case for Amnesty

Alfonso J. Damico

A University of Florida Book

The University Presses of Florida

Gainesville / 1975

Library of Congress Cataloging in Publication Data

Damico, Alfonso J.   1942–
    Democracy and the case for amnesty.

    (University of Florida social sciences monograph;
no. 55)
    "A University of Florida book."
    Includes bibliographical references.
        1.   Amnesty—United States. 2.   Vietnamese Conflict,
1961-   —United States. 3.   Amnesty. I.   Title.
II.   Series: Florida. University, Gainesville. University of Florida monographs: Social sciences;
no. 55.
DS559.8.A4D35   364.6   75-12502
ISBN 0-8130-0527-2

PRINTED BY THE STORTER PRINTING COMPANY, INCORPORATED
GAINESVILLE, FLORIDA

Acknowledgments

I want to thank the Graduate School of the University of Florida for a modest research grant that enabled me to begin this study. Through its program of grants, the university helps to translate research proposals into research activity. I also want to thank Professors David Spitz and David Kettler for teaching me that the study of political theory and a concern with the problems of men are part of the same enterprise. At an early stage, both of them read parts of the manuscript and encouraged me to continue with it. I am dedicating the study to my son Aaron.

Additional thanks must go to the University of Florida Graduate School for making possible the publication of this monograph.

Contents

1. Amnesty: Does Punishment Continue after the War?

T HIS ESSAY is a study of a perennial problem in political life—the conflict between the citizen's obligation to obey the law and his right, indeed his duty, to resist unjust laws. This conflict is especially acute in a democracy, since democracy alone imposes the peculiar requirement upon citizens that they both give and withhold their consent to authority. All men are to count equally in the making of the laws and, thus, they are all equally required to obey those laws. At the same time, the liberal tradition within democracy affirms that the individual is the final arbiter of when the law has violated the principles of democracy or a policy has transgressed the demands of decency—no matter how procedurally correct the methods whereby the policy is enacted. Like Thoreau, the democrat celebrates the conscientious man as the last barrier to acts of political barbarism by his government. But against Thoreau or the anarchist, the democrat also argues the advantages that men receive from their willingness to forgo their private decisions in favor of collective choices. By participating in the benefits made possible by the existence of a public authority, the individual indirectly acknowledges a general obligation to be law-abiding.

It is when the two goods of individual autonomy and public authority collide that personal tragedies and public problems occur. In America this was demonstrated by the government's conscription of its citizens to fight an unpopular war in Vietnam. It is in the public's response to the situation of those caught in the conflict between their attachment to their country but not to a particular government policy that we discover the character of the political community. So it is with an issue such as amnesty.[1]

1. Many of the issues in the amnesty debate were raised by various groups

The conflicts surrounding an idea such as amnesty can be seen as symbolic of certain classic and recurring problems in the life of a political community. These include the conflicts between conscience and law, political loyalty and other loyalties, punishment and setting aside prosecution. It is at this level of discussion that some of the deepest cleavages between philosophers occur. But these divisions are often only a more rigorous and complex reflection of the differences that divide public opinion. Further, in taking a stand for or against amnesty, one inevitably adopts one or another political posture—a set of beliefs about citizenship and authority. I have found it necessary and helpful, therefore, to enlarge my analysis of amnesty to include a discussion of the democratic community and the nature of loyalty to that community. Before evaluating the cases for and against amnesty, we need first to understand what it means to be a citizen in a democracy. For instance, underlying the case for amnesty after the Vietnam war is a view of democratic citizenship that can be shared by both supporters and opponents of that particular war. And although my discussion is not limited to the arguments for and against amnesty at the close of the Vietnam war, many of my observations are informed by that debate. I want, in other words, to talk about both civil disobedience and exiles in general, and about the American exiles created by the Vietnam war in particular. Sometimes I will argue for a general principle that I believe characterizes all civil disobedience and at other times I will defend a particular position that only applies to the actions of the Vietnam era exiles. It is important to my thesis that the reader keep this distinction in mind as he follows the argument.

The major political outlook embraced by amnesty's opponents is what I will call legalism.[2] Legalism is a rule-of-law model for resolving political conflicts. Its proponents teach the citizen that it is his duty not to judge the law but to obey it. Similarly, it requires public officials to exercise power in strict

---

in the public hearings before Senator Edward Kennedy's Administrative Practice and Procedure Subcommittee of the Senate Judiciary Committee, February 28–March 1, 1972 (*Selective Service and Amnesty*, 92d Cong., 2d sess., 1972).

2. I have borrowed this term from the book by Judith Shklar, *Legalism* (Cambridge, 1964). Shklar's critical analysis of the presuppositions underlying various philosophies of law has been of great help to me in thinking about law and politics as alternative models of conflict resolution.

conformity to rules fixed and announced beforehand so as to limit the arbitrary and capricious use of power. This is in many ways a persuasive teaching, protecting us from the twin dangers of official abuse of power and political anarchy. Legalism's major strength is its appreciation and defense of the values associated with being governed by laws and obligations rather than by threats and force. Justifying any disobedience requires some demonstration that the rule of law can, in fact, accommodate departures from the norm of obedience without undermining the continued vitality of that norm. Making such a justification highlights, I believe, certain critical weaknesses in legalism. Advocates of a rule-of-law model for understanding and managing social conflict tend to be insensitive to values other than law enforcement and to obscure the differences between political disputes and judicial questions by collapsing all conflicts into a question of legal right and wrong.[3]

Theories of justifiable civil disobedience are a major source of arguments supporting citizens' departures from the rule of law, and they provide important parts of my defense of amnesty. But amnesty's defense requires us to go beyond the more traditional accounts of civil disobedience. Unlike the more familiar disobedient citizen, war resisters who become exiles are unwilling to accept the legal consequences of their refusal to obey. Since theories of civil disobedience often differentiate principled from nonprincipled resistance by the willingness to accept arrest and punishment, an exile's evasion of punishment leads critics to question his conscientiousness. By evading punishment an exile's action also occasions greater alarm because the potential for disorder is greater when the disobedient citizen also defies the state's authority to judge him. Finally, in the case of Vietnam, those who opposed the war were selective conscientious objectors, opposed to a particular war but not to war in general, which means that theories justifying the conscience of the pacifist or the religious objector do not fit their case.

In puzzling over these problems, I soon discovered that two types of adjustments are necessary in the way that we normally discuss disobedience. While it is possible to draw various dis-

3. For another study of the dangers of legalism, see Otto Kircheimer, *Political Justice: The Use of Legal Procedure for Political Ends* (Princeton, 1961).

tinctions between the conscientious lawbreaker and the ordinary criminal, it is finally necessary to shift our attention away from the question of the "conscientiousness" of those who resist a particular war to the political context that occasions their resistance. When we are confronted with the individual lawbreaker such as a Thoreau or a Muhammed Ali, questions about his sincerity are perhaps important for determining what, if any, price he should pay for acting on his judgment. But when, as in the case of Vietnam, we are confronted with an entire group of dissenting citizens, the problem is less one of determining the sincerity of each and every resister than one of discovering how the democratic community can make room for a significant minority group so that the political good is so far as possible an inclusive good. In negotiating a settlement between a minority group—whether it is a striking labor union or a war resistance movement—and the larger society, the lawyer's art for assigning individual guilt or innocence is far less important than the political art of accommodation.[4]

The second adjustment that the reader will notice is a similarly practical or pragmatic one. Rather than attempting to construct a general theory of selective conscientious objection, I will ask if a society can grant a particular amnesty without seriously undermining the authority of the state. Would amnesty make it impossible for the society to fight future wars? Amnesty is a political issue demanding a calculation of the costs and benefits to the political system of withholding or granting it in a particular instance. By shifting the debate from the level of abstract legal and philosophical rules to the empirical level of likely consequences, it is possible to allay the fears of amnesty's opponents and to avoid those pernicious abstractions about the absolute value of law, on the one side, or the absolute value of conscience, on the other, that obscure the practical issue of amnesty's merits or drawbacks within an existing political situation.[5]

---

4. See Hannah Arendt's "Civil Disobedience," in her *Crises of the Republic* (New York, 1972). This essay is also in the collection of articles on obedience and disobedience edited by Eugene V. Rostow, *Is Law Dead?* (New York, 1971). See especially the comments on Arendt's essay in this volume by Edgar S. Cahn, pp. 243–49.

5. This second adjustment is guided by Quentin L. Quade's article "Selective

The original meaning of amnesty is "forgetfulness." It comes from the Greek word *amnestia*, which means the erasing from memory of past events.[6] Practically, amnesty is the legal oblivion of previous offenses. Amnesties differ from pardons in several ways. Pardons are granted on a case-by-case basis and are a nullification of punishment after there has already been a judicial determination of a person's guilt. A pardon is clearly an act of forgiveness; and although most amnesties have been granted with similar emphasis upon the state's "charity," amnesty literally is a decision not to judge past behavior. Pardons are normally included as part of an amnesty proclamation; those already in prison are pardoned along with those amnestied. All amnesties remove the threat of prosecution, but one must distinguish among amnesties. They may be universal or general, unconditional or conditional. A universal amnesty after the Vietnam war, for instance, would include resisters, evaders, deserters, and anyone in prison or under threat of prosecution for acts of civil disobedience in protest of the war. Indeed, a universal amnesty would also include a program to change the classification of those servicemen who received a less than honorable discharge because of their opposition to the war. In contrast, general amnesties exclude some persons from their benefits, although, as will be seen, the reasons for such discrimination are often arbitrary and vague. While an unconditional amnesty has no strings attached, a conditional amnesty requires the performance of some public service before the amnesty takes legal effect.

In the American legal system, there is no question about either the president or Congress possessing the power to extend an amnesty. The Constitution gives the president the "power to grant reprieves and pardons for offenses against the United States." Although various presidents had already interpreted the pardoning power to include the power of amnestying whole classes of people, it was only in 1872 that the Supreme Court ruled on the issue and agreed that the pardon power encom-

---

Conscientious Objection and Political Obligation," in *Obligation and Dissent*, ed. Donald W. Hanson and Robert Booth Fowler (Boston, 1971), pp. 336-56.

6. Both the *Encyclopedia Britannica* (1969) and the *Encyclopedia of the Social Sciences* (1930) have entries on the meaning of amnesty and some discussion of previous uses of the amnesty power, especially following international conflicts.

passed amnesties. The Court has also ruled that Congress has a similar amnesty power. Under the "necessary and proper" clause of the Constitution, Congress may enact an amnesty by remitting the penalties incurred under other national statutes. Presidential amnesties have been far more frequent, however, since they are easier to enact, simply requiring an executive proclamation. Depending upon how broadly amnesty is defined, there have been roughly a dozen presidential amnesty proclamations in American history, some major and some minor.[7]

As early as 1968, at the height of mass protests against the Vietnam war, some persons were talking about the possibility of an American amnesty at the end of that war. In December of that year several hundred persons made an appeal to President Johnson for a Christmas amnesty. Senator Eugene McCarthy, a leading critic of the Vietnam war, advocated a universal amnesty several times during his campaign for the 1968 Democratic presidential nomination. An antiwar group called "Clergy and Laymen Concerned about Vietnam" saw Henry Kissinger in 1969 to press upon the administration the desirability of a postwar amnesty.

It was not until the presidential election of 1972 that amnesty became something of a national issue. The Democratic party nominated an antiwar candidate, George McGovern, who declared early in his campaign, "If I am president when the war ends, I will extend an amnesty to those who on grounds of conscience have refused to participate in the Vietnam tragedy." McGovern was, however, opposed to a universal amnesty that would include deserters. Richard Nixon, the incumbent president who defeated McGovern in 1972, was opposed to any form of amnesty. At his January 31, 1973, news conference, for instance, he stated that the Vietnam war resisters and exiles had to pay the price of "a criminal penalty for disobeying the laws of the United States." By dismissing service in the Peace Corps as a "junket," he also objected to a conditional amnesty that would require alternative service.

7. A list of American amnesty proclamations and a summary of the Supreme Court cases interpreting the president's pardoning power can be found in The Constitution of the United States of America: Analysis and Interpretation, 88th Cong., 1st sess., 1964, pp. 456–61.

Despite the opposition of President Nixon to amnesty, a conditional amnesty of sorts was, in effect, operating for many of the war's opponents after 1970. As public disenchantment with the Vietnam war grew and the withdrawal of ground troops proceeded, the gap between the convictions of draft resisters and the public began to narrow. Judges around the country increasingly placed draft resisters on probation as long as they performed some alternative service. In 1967, only 10.4 per cent of those convicted for draft resistance received probation; in 1971 the figure stood at 62.7 per cent. Similarly, the military sharply increased its number of "general discharges" for de serters and soldiers refusing service in Vietnam. General di, charges, which are not nearly as punitive as dishonorable o bad conduct discharges, more than doubled in the Navy be tween 1969 and 1972. For many of the American exiles createc by the Vietnam war, their chief crime apparently was to be ahead of their fellow citizens in their resistance to the war.[8]

On September 16, 1974, President Gerald Ford announced a general and highly conditional amnesty for those who refused to serve in the Vietnam war. By this time America's direct military involvement in Vietnam had ended, and the previous president, Richard Nixon, had been forced to resign under threat of probable impeachment for his participation in what is known as the Watergate scandal. Under Ford's amnesty program, draft evaders or deserters who had not been convicted were given five months to turn themselves in to authorities, reaffirm their allegiance to the United States, and agree to spend up to two years in such public service jobs as hospital or conservation work. A Clemency Review Board was set up to review the cases of those already convicted for desertion or draft evasion to determine what service, if any, they must perform.

Initial reaction among the exiles to Ford's amnesty program

8. I have not talked directly about the exiles and their lives; they have told their own stories in a number of essays, magazines, and interviews. Roger Neville Williams has collected many of the stories of exiles living in Canada in *The New Exiles* (New York, 1971). A convenient collection of sixteen magazine articles describing the lives of deserters living in Paris and Stockholm has been published by Clergy and Laymen Concerned about Vietnam under the title *Deserters in Exile*. For a dramatic personal account of the desertion and return of one American soldier, see James Reston, Jr., *The Amnesty of John David Herndon* (New York, 1973). Also helpful is the magazine *Amex-Canada* published by American exiles in Canada.

was largely negative; many viewed the demand for alternative service as a form of punishment and a demand that the war's opponents admit that they were wrong. In the month following the amnesty proclamation, only a fraction of the evaders and deserters elected to participate in the program. Further, a legal oversight made it possible for deserters to avoid alternative service; they were to be given dishonorable discharges that would be changed to clemency discharges if they completed an alternative service. By electing to live with a dishonorable discharge, a deserter could avoid alternative service. These and other problems could have been avoided if the president had announced a universal and unconditional amnesty. Whether or not such an amnesty will eventually be proclaimed is unclear at this time, but the argument made here is that a universal and unconditional amnesty best accords with the democratic idea of limited loyalty to a limited state.

Amnesty is important not only for war resisters but for what it says about a people and their government. After Vietnam, amnesty was a chance to forget the offenses of a minority that refused to follow the majority in a direction from which the majority itself eventually turned away. By their actions the draft evaders and deserters forced Americans to re-evaluate the Vietnam adventure. Americans, like most people, have a strong tendency to "rally 'round the flag" in times of crisis and to accept with little questioning the government's definition of a "crisis." Minority disobedience has a role to play in changing this unreflective and automatic public response into the more critical and active one envisioned by the idea of democratic politics. In short, if a democratic society loses completely the conscience of resistance, it may lose democracy as well.

2. Democratic Loyalty

> For there is a point at which a state may
> attain such a degree of unity as to be no
> longer a state, or at which without actually
> ceasing to exist, it will become an inferior
> state, like harmony passing into unison, or
> rhythm which has been reduced to a single
> beat.
>
> Aristotle, *Politics*

> A theory of limited loyalty to limited
> government must recognize the sometime
> value of national disloyalty.
>
> Morton Grodzins, *The Loyal and the Disloyal*

THE VIETNAM war, the more militant protesters demanded, must be brought home to America. And the war often did come home. Dissent, political polarization, disobedience, the creation of an exile community, even the occasional bombing of a university building, a bank, or a Selective Service office, all must be figured into any assessment of the Vietnam war. The government, in turn, responded with political trials, accusations of disloyalty against dissenters, and an increase in the surveillance of vast numbers of citizens, including Congressmen. The Vietnam war became more than a problem of American foreign policy, it became a crisis for American democracy. Although the more obvious signs of the domestic crisis disappeared with the abolition of conscription and the end of American military participation in Vietnam, the lessons learned from that crisis are as important in the long run as the disappearance of the problem.

Most of the early explanations of that crisis focused upon the prolonged nature of the war, its origins, the powers of the president, and, more recently, the history of American cold war policy. But our problems also have roots in the very nature of

9

democracy. Democracy is a form of government that rests upon a complex network of multiple allegiances. The Vietnam war tested and frequently divided those allegiances by setting national loyalty against important non-national loyalties. Many citizens experienced the classical Aristotelian dilemma of how to be a good citizen, one who obeys the laws, when being a good man argued for disobedience to the laws. To see how this happened and to locate the role of amnesty as a response to such events, the idea of democracy needs to be brought out directly.

UNITY IN DIVERSITY

What separates naked force from legitimate and authoritative government is a widespread desire for the continuance of existing political arrangements. There must be some consensual base upon which the political structure rests and from which it draws support.[1] National loyalty is one idea that summarizes all of the ways in which men recognize that there is something "common" which binds them together and that membership in the inclusive community of the state is a good. This shared identity is easiest to achieve among small groups such as the Greek city-state, the clan, or the tribe. Such societies are closely integrated. The belief system is dominated by a single theology and a public philosophy that gives every aspect of life some meaning and defines each individual's role and place. The limited size of the population, a hunting or agricultural economy, and the kinship system conspire to unite the individual and the group. Whereas we confine politics to a fairly low level of importance in our daily lives, Aristotle, when searching for a definition of man, could sensibly say that "Man is a creature who lives in a polis." The polis has been described as "a living community, based on kinship, real or assumed—a kind of extended family, turning as much as possible of life into family life."[2] In circumstances of an intensive and encompassing communal spirit, national loyalty is a man's exclusive loyalty since

1. The links between politics and community are examined from a variety of angles in David W. Minar and Scott Greer, eds., The Concept of Community (Chicago, 1969).
2. H. D. F. Kitto, The Greeks (Baltimore, 1951), p. 78.

he identifies all of the other dimensions of his life, family, religion, and work, with the nation or, more accurately, the local geographical unit.

Man's progress has, however, been steadily in the direction of ever widening circles of association. Rather than a tight community based upon a single theology or public belief system, most men now live in multi-group societies with multiple-belief systems. The arrival of the city and then the nation-state has been accompanied by new religions, a new mobility, and competing ideologies. Industrial and technological advances transform the face of men's relationships as surely as they reshape the face of nature. Ease of migration, the new facility in communications, the spread of scientific, religious, economic, artistic, and even recreational associations, all are signs of the new pluralism in men's lives.

Critics often lament modern society's destruction of the seamless harmony of the small consensual community, labeling modern society a mass society. Such critics tend to exaggerate greatly the idyllic character of the closely knit community and to underestimate the immense liberation that has attended the arrival of the complex pluralist pattern of relationships. Instead of a life narrowly circumscribed by place and tradition (a member of the Bedouin tribe in Jordan sees travel outside of the tribal area as a curse descending from the forefathers to the child), the individual now moves in a world where these ties have loosened their grip. Similarly, authority in tribal communities is frequently rigidly hierarchical. Participatory democracy is as infrequent in uni-group societies as in modern pluralist ones. No modern man is, of course, totally free of tradition or the influence of surrounding groups upon him. But now there are many traditions and diverse groups to meet the needs and demands of diverse kinds of men. Thus, diversity has its roots in modern society as do the multiple loyalties that make unity a problem.

Perhaps no writer has done as much as the sociologist and political theorist Robert MacIver to explore the connections between the pluralism of society and democracy.[3] Refusing to

3. To characterize modern society as pluralist in the context of a discussion of democracy runs some risk. Unfortunately, political scientists have often obscured the character of the pluralist community by limiting their view of plu-

isolate one from the other or to insist that one causes the other, MacIver observes that every society needs both its techniques and its myths, i.e., the value-impregnated beliefs that it lives by and for. By techniques MacIver means all of the devices that men use to control and manipulate their natural and social environment. They include skills for easing toil, protecting advantages, securing more satisfactions, combatting enemies, and so forth. Techniques alone, however, will not account for the pattern of men's relationships. For example, both the United States and the Soviet Union have techniques of modern industrialism, but their property, control, and reward systems differ drastically. These differences can only be accounted for in terms of the varying myth systems that inform and sustain the life of each. The family is also an institution involving techniques of control and reward, but one myth system gives you matriarchy and another gives you patriarchy. As techniques change, men's myths change or are replaced by new ones.

Pluralism poses a new challenge for any code of authority. MacIver writes, "Not only under democratic conditions, but wherever modern industrial civilization extends, the nature of authority undergoes a transformation. A modern society, with its complexity of organization, becomes a multi-group society. It possesses no longer the homogeneity of culture that has pervaded the former types of society, even when they were sharply divided by class and caste. There is no longer one religion, one scale of values, one pervasive indoctrination. A multi-group society is a multi-myth society. Its appropriate form of government can be based only on some form of myth that accommodates conflicting myths . . . that condition is met by the myth of democracy."[4]

To appreciate the appropriateness of the nature of democracy as a response to the rise of pluralism, it is essential to keep clear the distinctions among society, community, and state. Yet political philosophers have frequently been so fascinated with

---

ralism to the decision-making machinery of politics to the neglect of what goes on outside of this system. MacIver has never made this error. For MacIver's writings on democratic pluralism, see especially *The Modern State* (New York, 1964), *The Web of Government* (New York, 1965), and David Spitz, ed., *Politics and Society* (New York, 1969).

4. *The Web of Government*, pp. 38–39.

the sovereignty of the new nation-state that these distinctions have been ignored. The consolidation of kingly power, the breakup of the universal church, the shifts in loyalty from family and region to the central political power, each contributed to the apparent moral as well as legal supremacy of the state.[5] Obedience to the state was now more than a convenience; for most men it had become a virtue. Men still suffer under the illusion that it is the chief virtue. But MacIver soberly reminds us that, "We live in communities; we do not live in states. We do not move and have our being in states, they are not integral things like communities. . . . Older languages, including ancient Greek, had no clear separate word when the reference was not to the state but to the community. 'Polis' meant equally the city and the city-state. . . . Yet the distinction, once it is brought to our attention, is surely obvious. Everywhere men weave a web of relationships with their fellows, as they buy and sell, as they worship, as they rejoice and mourn. This greater web of relationships is society, and a community is a delimited area of society. Within this web of community are generated many controls that are not governmental controls, many associations that are not political associations, many usages and standards of behavior that are in no sense the creation of the state. In the community develops the law behind the law, the multi-sanctioned law that existed before governments began and that the law of government can never supersede. Without the prior laws of the community all the laws of the state would be empty formulas. Custom, the first 'king of men,' still rules. The mores still prescribe. Manners and modes still flourish."[6]

Men have multiplied their associations for the simple reason that no one group, no single organization can provide for the needs and desires of different kinds of men. The comfort that a man receives from his family, the satisfaction that he discovers in his church, the comradeship offered by his club or his neighborhood gang are pleasures that do not depend upon the presence of the state's power. The state's intervention in man's communal life can easily become an unwarranted intrusion.

5. Cf. Joseph R. Strayer, On the Medieval Origins of the Modern State (Princeton, 1970), p. 56.
6. The Web of Government, p. 145; also see Spitz, Politics and Society, pp. 225–47.

Since a man lives in a network of sometimes reinforcing and sometimes conflicting allegiances, his commitment to one group or cause can never be complete or exclusive. A man with a single purpose is often the stuff of the dramatist's play, but such persons are rarely met in the world outside. Indeed, most of us are dismayed with someone whose total surrender to one experience leaves no room for qualified judgment or closes him off to new and unfolding relationships. The state is, indeed, more powerful than other groups and commonly expects of subjects their primary loyalty. What it can never expect without denying the facts of man's communal life is either that the political excludes the other dimensions of a man or that national loyalty is the only loyalty.

MacIver recognizes that when it is said that liberal democracy is a limited form of government something deeper is meant than just that there are checks and balances upon its power. Rather, democracy, and democracy alone, gives a constitutional sanction to the distinction between the community and the state. In such fashion democracy gives effect to the value of individuality or personality. Democracy destroys itself whenever it demands the total absorption of the individual within the state.

This does not mean that democratic citizens have no attachments that are more inclusive than the life of each association. But it is an attachment and unity bred of the recognition of diversity as a primary good. Philosophers have frequently worried over the links between the Particular and the Universal—the unit Man and the unity of association. Totalitarian writers and regimes postulate a superior One outside of the Many that annihilates the Many. Unity is sought in uniformity, order in coordination. Democracy, in contrast, affirms the Universal within the Particular. MacIver writes, "Not the perception of likeness, not alone what has been called the 'consciousness of kind' but also the way of life, the sense of common interests to be sustained by common endeavor, creates the unity of any group. The sense of the common over-rides the differences within the group but it does not abolish them. . . . normally the range of the common does not preclude the play of difference. The unity it sustains is not all-embracing. It admits many divergences of interest and of goal. . . . Since human beings are always variant the common is likely to be more securely established if its

guardians do not demand the complete conformity that con-
tradicts or suppresses such differences as are not irreconcilable
with the basic unity. The recognition of this fact is the major
insight of democracy."[7]

This general will for the state is linked to many things. Partly,
it is simply a matter of economics. While the single person is
subject to the caprice of nature, together men can control the
river's flooding or regulate the economic forces of supply and
demand. Custom also plays its part. As conservatives have
often noted, time tends to wrap any government in legitimacy.
Most men obey the government because it has never crossed
their minds not to obey; habit is as great a force in political
affairs as in daily routine. Psychologically, men often identify
"I" with "We," the individual self with the nation. The comfort
provided by the habitual and familiar usually means the comfort resulting from the ways of the nation where we happen to
have been born. Government services and manipulation of national symbols through holidays, songs, and rituals further
tighten the knot of individual-nation identification. Finally, sheer
prudence unites some men to the nation; disobedience is costly
and exile painful.

Democratic governments can rely upon these mechanisms as
a foundation for unity as easily as any other government. But
democracy is permanently barred from attempting to return to
the uni-group society. Democracy as a form of government
means tolerance, not only of political opposition but of the associational life of man within his communities. Democracy
either finds unity in diversity or it fails.

Bricks and Brickbats

In his helpful study *The Loyal and the Disloyal*, Morton Grodzins points out that democratic pluralism means that there is no
such thing as a *direct* national loyalty. He writes, "Life-
satisfactions are pursued and life-goals are achieved within
the framework of groups. . . . even where frames of reference
are derived from such apparent abstractions as the 'good of
mankind,' there is usually a face-to-face group in existence,

7. *The Web of Government*, p. 312.

functioning to define and to clarify abstract goals in terms of day-to-day activity. These are the sources of life's principal joys in a democratic state, and these are the objects of man's primary loyalties. . . . The welter of non-national loyalties makes a direct nation loyalty a misnomer. It does not exist. Loyalties are to specific groups, specific goals, specific programs of action."[8]

Thus we arrive at what might be considered the paradox of democracy. On the one hand, the multiplicity of beliefs and groups is the strength of democratic unity. Men tend to identify the many pleasures of life-satisfactions derived from non-national activities with the nation. But while non-national loyalties, to use Grodzins' language, are the bricks of national loyalty, they are also the brickbats of national disloyalty. Where men are serious members of groups other than the state, their commitments to the life of the association may lead them to break with the government.

Most discussions of pluralist citizenship have emphasized how it both protects the citizen from the state *and* binds him to it. The individual's membership in voluntary associations, it is pointed out, serves a variety of political functions. Through the sheer multiplication of numbers, it reduces the inequality involved in any confrontation between the individual and the state. Membership also enhances one's political skills and one's sense of political competency. The "joiner" is more likely to see the connections between public policies and his personal circumstances and to engage in action aimed at tipping the balance in his favor.

But group membership does more than encourage the citizen to press his claims against the state; it ties him closer to the state by including him, however modestly, in the public business. John Stuart Mill long ago pointed out that giving the individual some public function to perform or allowing him some participation in the state's affairs increases his feeling of obli-

---

8. (Chicago, 1956), pp. 28–29. Grodzins' discussion of democratic loyalty parallels many of the themes in MacIver's theory of democracy. Grodzins is particularly concerned to show that such government policies as the internment of Japanese-Americans during World War II can *create* disloyal citizens. On the various meanings of loyalty, cf. Robert Paul Wolff, "Analysis of the Concept of Political Loyalty," in *Political Man and Social Man*, ed. Robert Paul Wolff (New York, 1966), pp. 218–40.

gation toward the state. Participation is one of the most important ways that men learn to care for the state. Recent studies such as *The Civic Culture* have borne out Mill's insight by showing that support for the state increases with group membership and the attendant feeling of political efficacy.[9] Thus the democratic state's tolerance and protection of the group life of the community rebounds to its own advantage. The state can rely upon the community for support.

This is the ideal, or perhaps it should be called the idyllic, side of pluralism. For most men it is true that their associational life rarely (perhaps never) conflicts with their duty to the state. But there are times when a man's membership in a group, party, or movement or his identification with some reference group dedicated to opposition to a war can lead him to break with the state. Indeed, some contend that if his membership is genuine and his beliefs honest, he has a duty to honor these obligations against the state. Michael Walzer holds that "men have a *prima facie* obligation to honor the engagements they have explicitly made, to defend the groups and uphold the ideals to which they have committed themselves, even against the state, so long as their disobedience of laws or legally authorized commands does not threaten the very existence of the larger society or endanger the lives of its citizens. Sometimes it is obedience to the state, when one has a duty to disobey, that must be justified. First explanations are owed to one's brethren, colleagues, or comrades."[10] In short, as Walzer brings out, the more genuine pluralism there is in a democracy and the more men value their non-state associations and ideals, the more likely it is that upon occasion conflicts will occur that cannot be settled in the state's favor. Whether or not one sides with such men will depend upon many things—an estimation of the seriousness of the conflict between law and principle, command and conscience, and some calculation of whether the good accomplished by defiance of the law outweighs the good of law-abidingness. All that I have been concerned to argue up to this point is that there is no way for democracy to eliminate such conflicts without undermining the life of democracy itself.

9. Gabriel A. Almond and Sidney Verba, *The Civic Culture* (Boston, 1965).
10. *Obligations: Essays on Disobedience, War, and Citizenship* (Cambridge, 1970), pp. 16–17.

CONSCRIPTION AND CITIZENSHIP

Citizenship refers to the individual's membership in the more inclusive community of the state. This membership generates formal, moral, and felt obligations.[11] Formal obligation is legal; it refers to what the law and the constitution require of lawmakers, judges, policemen, and private citizens. By itself formal obligation is probably not very different from habit; that is, proscribed acts are avoided and prescribed behavior is forthcoming largely due to the adoption of appropriate roles. But formal obligation never stands alone; indeed, if it did, it would quickly collapse when faced with any challenge. Men must also feel obligated to follow the rules laid down by formal obligations. Formal and felt obligations are descriptive; one describes the expectations embedded in an institutional structure, the other describes when and how men come to feel obligated. For now, I am mainly concerned with felt obligations. But it is worth keeping in mind that from a moral viewpoint the fact that men feel obligated or that institutions define how public and private persons are expected to behave does not answer the question of whether these feelings and expectations are proper or "fitting." Technically, it is only the third variety of obligation, moral obligation, that appropriately refers to what a man "ought" to do, that is, what he is "obliged" to do. In other words, a man may feel obligated when he should not or, conversely, he may not feel an obligation that he morally has. And, of course, an account of the formal structure of institutions will tell us nothing about their justness.

Some of what has been said about democratic pluralism can easily be reinterpreted as forces leading to felt obligations. Gratitude for government benefits, the identification of life-satisfactions with the nation, participation in the political system, and belief in the idea of democracy can generate a feeling that compliance with the law is a duty.

Given the forces toward compliance, it is fairly simple to understand events that might lead to non-compliance. The extent to which the law invokes new demands, departs from familiar

11. Cf. Gray L. Dorsey, "Constitutional Obligation," in J. Roland Pennock and John W. Chapman, eds., *Political and Legal Obligation* (New York, 1970), pp. 179–213.

expectations, and requires new sacrifices is, perhaps, the most critical variable that increases the potential of non-compliance, of which more later. Non-compliance with law also results from conflicting obligations generated by membership in other associations. In the case of a young person who refuses induction or who deserts from the military for political reasons, non-compliance appears to begin with the absence of a felt obligation. This soon combines with a sense of obligation to others whose views the resister has come to share. He then becomes and often feels himself a member of the community of resisters. Non-compliance results from the feeling that personal life goals, formed by the groups that one belongs to, and the state's goals are totally disconnected.

Conscripting men to fight an unpopular war forces a wedge between the individual's formal obligation to be law-abiding and his feeling of being obligated, a feeling that formal obligations presuppose in order to be effective. For most men, conscription itself does not create this conflict. American governments have drafted men for military service for over a hundred years without major difficulties. Conscription will not account for the crisis of government authority during the Vietnam war. It is what men are asked to fight for that, at times, leads to challenges to the state's legitimacy. The Vietnam war, for instance, was a different type of war. Its origins for many were obscure; the reasons for fighting it seemed to vary from official to official and from month to month or from military campaign to military campaign. At one time Americans were encouraged to expect a military victory; at another moment military victory was dropped in favor of the more ambiguous, albeit more realistic, notion of political victory or preservation of presidential credibility. Whatever one's stand on the past wisdom of the Vietnam war, there is no longer room for dispute over the failure of the American government to make clear either the character or the purpose of the war. Government inconsistency breeds public disillusionment. And conscription seemed to many young men too high a price for citizenship when they could not see "why this is happening to me."

The tragedy of conscription is that it forces upon the individual an all-or-nothing choice. He must either risk dying for the state or defy the state. Yet, in many cases if it had not been for that particular war and that specific moment of conscription, many of the

Vietnam war resisters would have remained members of the American community. Life may be hell, to paraphrase Grodzins, but resistance is usually the last way out.

It is important to distinguish, in other words, between two types of resisters. There are some who press a total claim against the state; they deny the state's primacy in any area of their lives. These are revolutionaries. But the vast majority of the American exiles were young men who pressed only a partial claim against the state. They refused this service, denied the primacy of the state's claim in this instance. These were the rebels. Their loyalty to the state or, more precisely, to a particular government's policies was not total or unqualified. But their disloyalty was not total either. They still gave their loyalty to their wives, family, friends in the movement, and even the government in other matters. Above all, many were honoring their commitments to ideals which seemed to them threatened by the nation's actions. Indeed, many of the exiles relied upon these other loyalties to maintain them in a course contrary to the government's.

What needs to be remembered is that resistance and disobedience are directions that any democratic citizen might find himself following. Any person can be forced at some point to choose between the demands of his family, religion, and political beliefs and the demands of the state. Pluralist citizenship makes all of us obedient and disobedient, in the state and outside of the state.

REVOCABLE CONSENT

If democratic loyalty to the state must always be a limited loyalty, the wise course for the government is clear. It should make harmony and the interadjustment of men's various loyalties easy and conflict among them difficult. The web of order characteristic of democracy is most secure where the state does not place national loyalty in competition with other loyalties.

Perhaps all of this is less true when the contest is simply between the state and a single individual. But where the number of people opposing and disobeying government draft laws increases to tens of thousands, the government has failed to understand the consensus necessary for democracy to work. The presumption, which I normally share, that law-abidingness is the individual's first duty can no longer be maintained when dissent assumes the proportions of a minority group opposition. *The isolated lawbreaker casts suspicion upon himself. A community of resisters casts suspicion upon the government.* This difference was appreciated long ago by the major philosopher of American liberal democracy, John Locke. Responding to charges that the teaching that government derives its powers from the consent of the governed would encourage disobedience and rebellion, Locke wrote, "To this, perhaps, it will be said, that the people being ignorant and always discontented, to lay the foundation of government in the unsteady opinion and uncertain humour of the people, is to expose it to certain ruin. . . . To which I answer, quite the contrary. People are not so easily got out of their old forms as some are apt to suggest. They are hardly to be prevailed with to amend the acknowledged faults in the frame they have been accustomed to. . . . Nor let any one say that mischief can arise from hence as often as it shall please a busy head or turbulent spirit to desire the alteration of the government. 'Tis true such men may stir whenever they please, but it will be only to their own just ruin and perdition. For till the mischiefs be grown general, and the ill designs of the rulers become visible, or their attempts sensible to the greater part, the people, who are more disposed to suffer than right themselves by resistance, are not apt to stir. The examples of particular injustice or oppression of here and there an unfortunate man moves them not. But if they universally have a persuasion grounded upon manifest evidence that designs are carrying on against their liberties, and the general course and tendency of things cannot but give them strong suspicions of the evil intention of their governors, who is to be blamed for it? Who can help it if they, who might avoid it, bring themselves into this suspicion?"[12]

I have deliberately anticipated in these last few paragraphs some of the further concerns that will arise in the discussion of the merits of amnesty. Locke reminds us that if consent is to be meaningful in a democracy, it must always be revocable. Otherwise, it becomes mere custom or habit, which is an in-

---

12. "Second Treatise on Civil Government," in *Social Contract*, ed. Ernest Barker (New York, 1969), pp. 129–33.

effective restraint upon the state's power. When consent is withdrawn by an isolated individual here and there, it is likely to remain a legal rather than a political and public problem. But when consent is withdrawn by large numbers, attention must shift from the legal forum to the political arena. Finally, Locke cautions us against assuming that once you tell men that political reality is a created reality or that political order is their order, you run the risk of continuous disorder. What is impressive about man's history is not how quick he is to say no, but how tolerant he is of abuses that would often justify his refusal. Men go to considerable lengths to smooth out any conflicts between their loyalty to the nation and other loyalties. They grumble; they accept the state's demand as a sacrifice that they must pay; they tell themselves that "they," meaning those in government, know best. Men, in effect, often do ask what they can do for the state rather than ask what the state can do for them. Given men's aversion to disobedience, does not the government bear much of the burden for bringing "themselves into this suspicion"? A major responsibility of any democratic government is to evaluate the likely effects of its policies upon the social agreement necessary for the rule of law to work. When its policies are such as to undermine the widespread public agreement to be rule-following, it must accept much of the blame for the divisions within the country. It must also pick up the responsibility for reconciling those divisions.

3. Amnesty and Its Uses

THE LIFE of the individual and the life of the community are interdependent. Both are sustained by mutual rights and duties, mutual aid, shared beliefs, and a sense of loyalty. This network of allegiances between the individual and the group and among groups is often the source of men's greatest comforts and pleasures. Yet precisely because it is a complex and changing network rather than a uniform and invariable pattern, it can be broken. Competing religions, racial divisions, conflicting ideologies, economic crises, changing images of man himself, the acquisition of new loyalties or changes in the old ones, all can set individual against group or group against group.

Why men come into conflict, however, is not the topic of this chapter. Rather, it is about the role that amnesty can play in aiding or simply signaling the end of the conflict. Although history cannot decide political and moral arguments, it can indicate what men have proven capable of in the past and show how they have acted in circumstances that bear some rough resemblance to our own.

In looking at previous uses of amnesty, one discovers six different ways that it has been employed.

After a successful political rebellion, an amnesty may be granted to the supporters of the overthrown government. Such an amnesty will likely exclude the leaders of the government from its benefits.

Military deserters may be offered amnesty upon the condition that they return to their military units. Such an amnesty is likely to have little appeal to those who have deserted for political reasons rather than for reasons of personal comfort.

Peace treaties ending international conflicts normally include the extension of an amnesty by each side to the citizens of the other country for offenses each has committed against the other.

Although less frequent, a government may provide amnesty for its own citizens compromised by their behavior during an international conflict. When this has occurred, the amnesties have included forgiveness for offenses such as spying or giving information to the enemy that are far more serious than draft evasion or military desertion.

At the end of a civil war, the victorious government may extend an amnesty to the former rebels.

Amnesties may or may not include pardons for those already convicted or under indictment for political offenses. Governments normally exclude such persons from the benefits of the amnesty, extending pardons to such men on a case-by-case basis.

In most of these circumstances, amnesty is an act taken after the military conflict has ended. When a government again feels secure or a new one has been firmly established, attention shifts to the problem of cementing the military resolution with a political reconciliation.

THE GREEK AMNESTY OF 403 B.C.

Among the earliest decisions to wipe out the recollection of past political events, the best recorded one is the Athenian amnesty of 403 B.C.[1] It provides us with the first clear example of the form and content of the amnesty concept. Although exact dates and some of the details of the amnesty are in dispute, the major events surrounding its issuance are clear enough.

In 404 B.C. an oligarchical group consisting of leaders from the wealthiest class and the military successfully consolidated its control of Athens' government. The oligarchs proceeded to deal harshly with political opposition, even resorting to murder. Political participation was restricted to members of the highest class. Many of the democrats opposed to the government fled

1. Alfred P. Dorjohn, *Political Forgiveness in Old Athens: The Amnesty of 403 B.C.* (Evanston, 1946); Aristotle, *Constitution of Athens*, xxxvii–xxxix.

into exile in the mountains north of Athens. Civil war then broke out between the two groups, and although each side sought allies among the other Greek city-states, the conflict remained predominantly a clash between the rebels and the state. The government's military campaigns against the rebels were unsuccessful, and the lack of citizen enthusiasm for the war and the harsh rule of the government at home combined to undermine the oligarchs' power. According to Aristotle, the original Board of Ten, the governing body, was replaced by a group committed to ending the struggle. It was at this point that the democratic party offered an amnesty to the other side, thereby easing the way for the government to end the fight. The granting of the amnesty and the return of the exiles apparently coincided. The rebels did not desire to continue the fight beyond the point at which the oligarchical government had to step down. The amnesty was widely viewed as an assertion that the Athenian community was finally more important than the divisions of the war.

Initially, the amnesty was simply a political agreement between the two warring factions, although the rebels were in a position to press for a total and punitive victory. Every Athenian citizen took an oath upholding the agreement; the oath was later supplemented by an act that made the amnesty a law. In supporting the amnesty, leaders in the democratic party urged citizens to abide by the spirit as well as the letter of the law. Much of the success of the amnesty is traced to the mood of reconciliation encouraged by Athens' new leaders.

The amnesty stated that previous political events were legally forgotten. Specific measures provided that informers would not be prosecuted for their behavior during the war; confiscated property was returned, where possible, to its rightful owners; legal action to recover money was allowed, but no suits could be brought for damages resulting from the war. Finally, for those still fearful or disaffected from the democratic government, provision was made allowing them to emigrate. Although violations did occur—for example, some persons were brought to trial for damages—all commentaries report that the amnesty earned the Athenians the admiration of the other Greek cities.

The Athenians operated under many advantages. The small size of the city-state, the need to unite against outside enemies, the short duration of the conflict, and the intense feeling of common citizenship found among the Greeks contributed to the success of the reconciliation. But it must also be kept in mind that a civil war that sets "brother against brother," as one Greek writer described the conflict, often creates greater bitterness and resentments than a conflict between two countries where brothers fight strangers.

INTERNATIONAL CONFLICTS

Since the seventeenth century, amnesties have become so regular a part of the peace treaties ending international wars that amnesty is assumed to be a part of such treaties unless provision is explicitly made to the contrary.[2] There are numerous examples of both sides in a war extending amnesty to the citizens of the other. One of the last acts of business at the Congress of Vienna in 1815 was an amnesty for the Poles and Swedes. The conclusion of the war between Russia and Turkey in 1878 had the novel feature of requiring Turkey to give amnesty to its own citizens who were disloyal during the war. Although the treaties ending World War II did not contain general amnesty clauses, France, Germany, Norway, the Netherlands, Belgium, and Japan passed amnesties for their own citizens guilty of political offenses during the war. Such amnesties freed millions from the threat of prosecution. A major blot in the history of amnesty proclamations was the Russian government's execution of several sailors who took part in the Potemkin sailors' revolt of 1905, despite the promise of amnesty for them.

The most recent gesture of political magnanimity by a government occurred after the French Algerian conflict. In the early 1960s, Europeans, especially large numbers of Frenchmen, living in Algeria revolted against DeGaulle's plans for Algerian independence. In 1961 four retired French generals led a three-day revolt against the French government in Algeria, defying DeGaulle's Algerian program. Yet DeGaulle issued an amnesty proclamation for the supporters of the officers and later pardoned

---

2. See the entries on amnesty in the *Encyclopedia Britannica* (1969) and in the *Encyclopedia of the Social Sciences* (1930).

the officers also. DeGaulle thus forgave acts far more serious than draft evasion or nonviolent disobedience to the state.

AMERICAN AMNESTIES

United States presidents have issued approximately ten amnesty proclamations, both conditional and unconditional, some major and some relatively minor ones.[3] The first experience with amnesty in this country dates back to the Whiskey Rebellion of 1794. Farmers in western Pennsylvania refused to pay the new whiskey excise and violently resisted the tax collectors. The national government viewed resistance to the tax as a direct challenge to its authority, a view pressed most vigorously upon President Washington by Alexander Hamilton. Washington was persuaded to take strong measures against the farmers. Raising an army larger than the troops he commanded during most of the war with England and leading them himself into Pennsylvania, Washington demonstrated the seriousness with which the government viewed the confrontation. This show of strength was sufficient to cause the collapse of the resistance, and the tax soon was paid.

Having demonstrated the power of the new government, Washington also set the precedent for political reconciliation through amnesty. By issuing an amnesty on July 10, 1795, for those who had defied the government, he set the tone for many of those who have argued for amnesties for other types of political offenders: "Though I shall always think it a sacred duty to exercise with firmness and energy the constitutional powers with which I am vested, yet my personal feeling is to mingle in the operations of the Government every degree of moderation and tenderness which justice, dignity, and safety may permit."[4]

Four years later, President John Adams appeared to follow Washington's example by granting "a full, free and absolute pardon to all and every person concerned in said insurrection." Thus, resistance to the national government, again occurring in Pennsylvania, ended on a note of forgiveness. Adams' tone,

3. For a complete listing of presidential and Congressional acts of amnesty and pardon, see the table in *Selective Service and Amnesty*, pp. 668–69.

4. James D. Richardson, *A Compilation of the Messages and Papers of the Presidents: 1789–1902* (New York, 1897–1907), 1:184; the proclamation is at p. 181.

however, was less one of reconciliation than of the charity of the powerful toward, in his words, "the ignorant, misguided, and misinformed in the counties [who] have returned to a proper sense of their duty." Adams' proclamation also excluded those already tried and found guilty or those under indictment.[5]

Four early presidents issued severely conditional amnesties for American military deserters. In 1807 Jefferson granted amnesty to any deserters as long as they returned to their military units within four months.[6] Later, Madison, on three separate occasions, proclaimed amnesties that employed much the same language as Jefferson's.[7] Perhaps the most unusual pardon of military deserters was Andrew Jackson's directive to the War Department to pardon deserters upon the condition that they never again serve in the military.

All of these early presidential acts wandered considerably from amnesty's literal meaning of forgetfulness. Like Adams, Washington described the subjects of his proclamation as "misguided." While the amnesties set aside legal prosecution, the offenders were, nevertheless, pronounced guilty. Such punitive amnesties can be contrasted with nonpunitive ones where the government acknowledges as at least reasonable the complaints of the dissenters. This distinction becomes clearer when these early amnesties are compared with the amnesties issued during the American Civil War.

The Civil War was America's first experience with large numbers of conscripted soldiers. During the war, Lincoln adopted a policy toward Union deserters and resisters very similar to those of earlier presidents.[8] They were promised amnesty on the condition that they rejoin their regiments. Lincoln's early policy was a mixture of harsh threat and measures intended to moderate the punishment of deserters. On one hand, he warned deserters that failure to return would lead to strict punishment upon their arrest. On the other, he directed the War Department in 1864 to make sure "that the sentence of all

---

5. Ibid., 1:303-4.
6. Ibid., 1:425.
7. Ibid., 1:512, 514, 543.
8. An exhaustive study of amnesties and pardons during the Civil War period is Jonathan Truman Dorris, *Pardon and Amnesty under Lincoln and Johnson* (Chapel Hill, 1953).

deserters who have been condemned by court-martial to death
. . . be mitigated to imprisonment during the war. . . ."[9] Although the war was over the very existence of the Union itself,
no action was taken by Lincoln after the war against either
draft evaders or military deserters.

This policy of reconciliation was even more evident in Lincoln's, and later Johnson's, policies toward the participants in
the rebellion. Both found in the course of political forgetfulness
the best guarantee that bitter political differences would not
continue to threaten the nation's political health.

The Civil War did produce, however, its advocates of severe
punishment. For many, the issue was clear: the Confederates
were in open rebellion and thus guilty of treason. In contrast,
Lincoln viewed the rebellion as something more than or different from the crime of treason.[10] In rejecting the view that
defined the South's rebellion as more criminal than political,
Lincoln stated as his highest goals the preservation of the
Union and a settlement of the conflict that would bring the
South back into the Union as a working member rather than
just as a defeated enemy. Toward these ends, he issued various
amnesty proclamations for those participating directly or indirectly in the rebellion upon the condition that they reaffirm
their allegiance to the Union.[11] On December 8, 1863, he used
his pardoning power to declare that all prosecution of rebelling
citizens would be set aside and their property, except in slaves,
would be fully restored.[12] The proclamation was not universal
in that it excepted certain classes of persons such as high military officers and the major civil leaders of the Confederacy. But
even those persons were invited to seek pardons on a case-by-
case basis. Keeping in mind that battles were still being waged,
Lincoln's liberal use of executive pardon and amnesty stands
as a high mark in the history of political reconciliation.
Through his proclamation Lincoln did a great deal to modify
some of the more extreme measures demanded by those north-
erners who were in an avenging mood during and after the war.

---

9. Richardson, 6:233.
10. Dorris, p. 5. For some of the more ridiculous and inhuman proposals for
punishing the Confederate President Jefferson Davis, see ibid., pp. 282–83.
11. Richardson, 6:102–4, 188–89, 213–15.
12. Ibid., 6:213.

Whether or not Lincoln would have granted a universal amnesty at the close of the war cannot definitely be known. His untimely death left the final settlement of the amnesty issue to President Johnson, yet Lincoln evidently had such a proclamation in mind. Charles Sumner, reporting on a conversation that he had with Lincoln shortly before his death, reports that Lincoln "was not for a moment tempted into any remark indicating any desire to punish even Jefferson Davis. In refutation to a statement that Davis should be hanged Lincoln said again and again, 'Judge not, that ye be not judged.' "[13] In his last public speech, Lincoln hinted that he was contemplating a much broader amnesty proclamation for the South, saying that he would act when the time seemed proper. Further, Lincoln's last cabinet meeting, which was held to consider a general plan of reconstruction for the South, found him in a forgiving mood. Gideon Welles who attended the meeting wrote in his diary that the president "was particularly desirous to avoid the shedding of blood or any vindictiveness of punishment. He gave plain notice that morning that he would have none of it. No one need expect that he would take any part in hanging or killing these men, even the worst of them. 'Frighten them out of the country, open the gates, let down the bars, scare them off,' said he, throwing up his hands as if scaring sheep. 'Enough lives have been sacrificed; we must extinguish our resentments if we expect harmony and union.' "[14]

Lincoln's course was clear—promote unity by offering to erase the recollection of previous political events. The decision to pursue this course was left to his successor, Andrew Johnson. What is remarkable about Johnson's decision to follow a direction very similar to Lincoln's is that everything seemed to indicate that he would be a vengeful president. When southern senators made their farewell speeches upon the secession of their states, Johnson as vice president had answered "Were I the President . . . I would do as Thomas Jefferson did in 1806 with Aaron Burr, who was charged with treason. I would have them arrested and tried for treason; and if convicted, by the Eternal God, I would see that they suffered the penalty of the

13. Edward L. Pierce, *Memoirs and Letters of Charles Sumner* (Boston, 1877–93), 4:239.
14. Gideon Welles, *Diary* (New York, 1960), 2:298.

law at the hands of the executioner."[15] Yet before his term in office was over, Johnson issued no less than four amnesty proclamations.[16]

Johnson's first amnesty proclamation of 1865 was a reissuance of Lincoln's offer of amnesty to those participating in the rebellion upon condition that they accept the legitimacy of the national government. This amnesty did reflect Johnson's initially more punitive attitude in that he greatly expanded the number of persons excluded from it. But his next three proclamations became increasingly more generous. At the end of the war, he issued an amnesty sharply reducing the number of excluded classes: only leading military and political figures were denied its benefits. A year later the exemptions were further reduced to exclude only those under current indictment for treason.

On December 25, 1868, after three years in office, Johnson announced to the country what has become known as the Christmas amnesty. It was a universal and unconditional amnesty for all persons who had taken part in the rebellion, and it included a full pardon for all those imprisoned for political acts during the war. The legal memory of the war was now officially and totally wiped out. Johnson finally completed the purpose announced at the time of his very first proclamation. He stated, "a retaliatory or vindictive policy attended by unnecessary disqualifications, pains, penalties, confiscations and disfranchisements, now as always, could only tend to hinder reconciliation among the people and national restoration. . . ."[17] It took Johnson three years, but he came to recognize that reconciliation requires an unqualified act of good faith that removes any doubt about the intentions of the government toward its former opponents.

Many other things combined to move Johnson from his earlier support of strict punishment to one of leniency. Lincoln's legacy, the influence of Lincoln's former secretary of state and later friend of Johnson, William Seward, and the sincerity of the former rebels in their desire to return to the Union were factors in Johnson's commitment to amnesty. Whatever John-

15. *Congressional Globe*, 36th Cong., 2d sess., pp. 1354–56, cited by Dorris, p. 96.
16. Richardson, 6:310–12, 547–49, 655–56, 708.
17. Ibid., 6:548.

son's final reasons, there can be little doubt that his pursuit of the course pointed by Lincoln did as much as anything else to make the persistence of the Union a social and political fact as well as a military one.

The Civil War experiment with amnesty provides today's citizen with mixed counsel. The Vietnam war resisters, it is true, were not in the same category as defeated combatants in a civil war. Neither Lincoln nor Johnson extended an amnesty to Union citizens or soldiers who disobeyed the government or refused its support. The policy here, as has been noted, was to offer deserters a chance to rejoin the army, and after the war the government adopted an informal policy of simply ignoring the whole issue of apprehending and punishing evaders and deserters. Thus, the Civil War does not provide us with a historical precedent for the formal removal of the threat of prosecution for citizens disobedient to the immediate government under whose jurisdiction they find themselves.

The inexactness of the analogy must not be pushed too far. Once the former rebels were again under the jurisdiction of the national government, they were still amnestied. More important, the relevance of the Civil War analogy turns upon the resemblance between the alternative attitudes the government can adopt toward those who have broken with it for political rather than criminal reasons. We have more to learn from the spirit than from the form of the Civil War amnesty proclamations. To learn this lesson it is necessary to distinguish, as did Lincoln, between crimes and unlawful political acts. So long as resistance is equated with ordinary crime, the language of the law—innocence and guilt, trial and punishment—obscures the political factors in those situations where the conflict is over the law itself. In dealing with the criminal, the representative of the law is accustomed to asking whether or not a law has been broken and whether or not this person is guilty of the violation. This was, in effect, the attitude of those who criticized Lincoln as a "pardoning president." Lincoln's leniency toward the South, I suggest, can be accounted for by his judgment that the rebellion was more than a crime. The illegality of the South's secession was incidental to the political reasons behind that secession. As president, Lincoln acted neither as a lawyer preoccupied with rules of law nor as a judge seeking to adjudicate individual blame or innocence, but as a politician attempting to negotiate a political settlement. Amnesty and pardon were part of Lincoln's negotiating tactics. Lincoln's choice prevailed over those who demanded a strict accounting before the judge's bench. Is there anyone who doubts that his was the proper and wiser course?

THE STRUGGLE FOR AMNESTY AFTER TWO WORLD WARS

During this century, amnesty campaigns in America have been waged following both world wars.[18] Dissent during the two wars was mainly centered among pacifist groups. The largest number imprisoned in World War I were conscientious objectors who could not meet the narrow requirement of the 1917 Selective Service Act that limited conscientious objector status to members of a "well-recognized religious sect or organization at present organized and existing and whose existing creed or principles forbid its members to participate in war in any form. . . ." No provision was made for members of such sects who might also object to noncombatant service in support of war. Persons whose objections to war were rooted in political, philosophical, or even religious principles and were not members of a recognized peace church, were thus excluded. No exemption was, of course, made for those whose objections were to a particular war rather than to war itself. Yet the number of objectors during the war remained small. The number denied conscientious objector status and imprisoned in camps was around four thousand. Others imprisoned included those who refused to register at all, men arrested for a variety of political offenses, including the urging of pacifist and other "radical" views, and members of the American Socialist Party who refused to support the war effort.

The mood of the country during World War I was one of harshness, making any form of political dissent risky. Nothing illustrates this better than the imprisonment of Eugene Debs, leader of the Socialist party. In 1918 Debs was convicted and sentenced to ten years in prison for delivering a speech against the war, a decision upheld by the Supreme Court. At the time

18. See Mulford Q. Sibley and Philip E. Jacob, *Conscription of Conscience* (Ithaca, 1952), chaps. 17 and 20.

of the armistice ending the war, Debs and nine hundred others still remained in American prisons. The goal of the amnesty campaign that emerged following the war was to have Debs and all other political prisoners released. Technically, it was a struggle for pardon, since its focus was upon those already tried and imprisoned.

The campaign was organized by the National Civil Liberties Bureau, forerunner of the American Civil Liberties Union, and the Socialist party. Efforts to persuade President Wilson to grant a pardon were doomed from the outset. He viewed critics of the war as traitors and vowed that they would never be set free during his administration. Yet, other Allied governments began to free their political prisoners shortly after the war's end. Italy, France, Canada, and Belgium issued formal pardons and amnesty proclamations for opponents of the war. England pardoned most of its prisoners, although no general amnesty was granted. In America, however, the sixty-five-year-old Debs was not pardoned until Christmas Day, 1921, by Warren Harding. Other political prisoners were not released until pardoned by Coolidge in 1924, over six years after the war.

While the first amnesty campaign of this century succeeded eventually in securing the release of political prisoners, it failed to win a general amnesty for those who remained under the threat of prosecution. Although none of the dissenters were guilty of any crimes against persons or property, the American public and its presidents refused to wipe from memory the political actions of those individuals whose consciences had come into conflict with the authority of the state.

For most Americans, World War II was seen as a necessary struggle to defeat an aggressive enemy that was a threat to human decency as well as international peace. Enlistments were high and support for the war overshadowed what opposition to it did exist. Draft resistance and desertion were never major problems. Conscientious objectors, however, still found themselves faced with either meeting a narrow test of religious exemption or serving time for their beliefs. At the time of Japan's surrender three thousand objectors were still in prison, and the total number of Selective Service violators in prison at the war's end was 15,805, a significant but small number when compared to the number who served. An effort to win a presidential amnesty for conscientious objectors was under way shortly after the defeat of Japan. Very soon, the goal became a general amnesty for all prisoners and those under threat of prosecution. Although the campaign was usually fought in terms of gaining a pardon for prisoners, an amnesty proclamation would have freed all classes of offenders, those out of prison as well as those already imprisoned. For two years, the struggle was carried on through picketing, petitions, and fasts by prominent leaders of the amnesty movement.

The American public, according to a Gallup poll taken in 1946, favored amnesty for conscientious objectors by a 69 per cent majority; 23 per cent were opposed, and 8 per cent held no opinion. Supporters of the amnesty campaign, however, wanted all Selective Service violators amnestied. Leading newspapers in the country supported a general amnesty and in some cases a universal amnesty that would include deserters. There were some papers, however, that voiced strong objections. The *Kansas City Star* editorialized: "For every conscientious objector behind bars there are thousands of well-remembered graves of American youths who died defending their country, and other thousands of disabled men. . . . The men who were entirely willing to sacrifice our freedom in the name of conscience have a doubtful claim on the nation's mercy."[19]

President Truman ruled out the possibility of a general amnesty from the very beginning. He told a group of representatives from the Jehovah's Witnesses that he was a "fighting man" who had little sympathy for those who would not fight for their country. But as support for the amnesty campaign appeared to be gaining strength, some response was needed from the White House. Truman finally acted by appointing a three-member Amnesty Board to review the cases of the political prisoners and to make recommendations to him for executive clemency. Following the work of this board, Truman issued a proclamation on December 23, 1947, that was a harsh defeat for the proponents of amnesty. Truman's so-called amnesty did not pardon all violators, not even all conscientious objectors. Rather, it was a pardon for 1,523 of the 15,805 men in prison. The remaining prisoners had to await their release through either parole or the serving out of their sentences.

The 1,523 men chosen for pardon were selected by the Am-

19. Quoted ibid., p. 393.

nesty Board. There were many immediate and specific complaints about its decisions. The board refused to consider the case of any man with a previous criminal record, but it failed to explain why such past behavior should affect a judgment about his failure to support the war. It also automatically excluded most of the ten thousand men who were in prison for reasons other than a denial of a request for conscientious objector status. Among conscientious objectors, it was willing to consider only the cases of those who might meet the religious principles test. For many of its critics, it again acted arbitrarily in deciding which religious groups were to be recognized as legitimate and which ones were not—excluding, for example, Jehovah's Witnesses, many of whom were still in prison. More broadly, critics charged the board with failing to understand the very nature of amnesty. Instead of a case-by-case pardoning process, amnesty is intended to apply to whole classes of people. But neither Truman nor the board was ready to go this far. Harold Ickes, at one time Franklin Roosevelt's secretary of the interior, voiced the dismay of many advocates of amnesty by writing in a *New York Post* column that "Like Shylock, insisting upon the last shred of his pound of flesh, certain people seem intent on inflicting on these unfortunates the last measure of the law. I, for one, protest against such harsh inflexibility. President Truman found it easy to pardon members of the Pendergast gang who had been convicted of vote frauds in a Missouri election. And after all, the theft of votes is a deadlier assault upon American institutions than an aversion to war. Can we no longer forgive? Has the gentle quality of mercy dried up in our hearts?"[20]

Given the experience of the Amnesty Board following World War II, any plan for a case-by-case review of those in exile or in prison as a consequence of their opposition to a particular war can be expected to encounter numerous difficulties. A Clemency Review Board, for example, faces the difficult task of developing criteria for deciding to whom to grant amnesty without working an injustice in other cases. If a demand for alternative service varies according to mitigating factors, how does one decide the relative weight to be assigned to the fact that a deserter has

---

20. November 13, 1945.

already completed a tour of military duty in a combat zone and the fact that a draft resister has been in exile for over seven years? An examination of men's motives, so as to discriminate between the conscientious and nonconscientious resister, is likely to result in a bias that favors the educated and articulate over those who cannot intellectualize their motives. Even if a war resister states that he deserted for personal reasons rather than because of opposition to the war, is it clear that he would have deserted had it not been for the climate of opinion created by widespread opposition to the war that he was being asked to fight? A major advantage of a universal and unconditional amnesty is that it avoids these imponderables and a protracted administrative process that can easily delay for years the removal of the threat of criminal prosecution from those whose political and moral convictions were genuine.

CONCLUSIONS

Earlier amnesties have not affected America's subsequent ability to raise an army or to wage a war successfully. As Henry Steele Commager has insisted, the large numbers of draft resisters and deserters during the Vietnam war were less a commentary upon their character than upon the nature of the war.[21] Other governments that amnestied their political prisoners following the world wars have experienced no weakening in national loyalty.

Any consideration of political offenses and punishment must keep in mind that a government's decision to go to war entails the greatest demand that it can normally make of a citizen—asking him to risk dying for the state. As a democracy, America should not merely tolerate but insist that the citizen ask the state to explain clearly the connection between his potential sacrifice and the things that he, along with other citizens, values. Some men, of course, will always refuse the state's demand. They are the pacifists, the philosophical anarchists, those simply incapable of killing, and the alienated. Others will always respond to the demand regardless of the conflict or the state's reasons. They include the unreflective believers in "My country

21. "The Case for Amnesty," *New York Review of Books*, April 6, 1972, pp. 23–25.

right or wrong" and, tragically, those for whom war is an escape from the boredom of their normal lives or a chance to prove their manliness.

Those always willing to march off to war clearly present no problem to the state (their threat to the democratic ideal of conscientious citizenship is another matter). Conscientious objectors to all wars are becoming less of a difficulty as the Supreme Court expands the test for conscientious objection to include philosophical as well as religious beliefs. There is, however, another group of men who refuse to fight in some wars. They do not deny that men acquire an obligation to die or kill for the state; they only deny that that obligation is absolute. Their opposition is not to bearing arms, but to using them against a particular people, or in defense of an erroneous principle or lack of principle. It is this group that raises the most serious issues that must be confronted. Many are among democracy's most conscientious and discriminating citizens. That is, they hold neither an indiscriminate rejection of all wars nor an indiscriminate enthusiasm for all wars. They could agree with the British philosopher Bertrand Russell, who, when chided for his support of World War II since he had been imprisoned for his objections to World War I, stated, "I like to choose my wars." Yet these are the people most likely to come into conflict with the state's authority. America has increasingly come to grips with religious and philosophical conscientious objectors; it must now see if it can understand and make room for political conscientious objectors.

4. Objections to Amnesty and Their Fallacies

In THIS chapter I will examine the case against amnesty as it appeared, following the Vietnam war, in journals, newspapers, and public hearings. I have, however, gone further than many of these criticisms of amnesty by examining some of the literature on civil disobedience that seemingly supports the brief against amnesty. Before moving to the arguments against amnesty, a preliminary remark might help the reader to see the general direction to be taken. A full response to the objections to amnesty cannot be separated from a presentation of the reasons for amnesty. The final case for amnesty, in other words, must be a positive one, not simply a critique of the other side. This positive case is taken up in the next chapter, but before that, something else needs to be done. If there were, as some do argue, an absolute prohibition against ever breaking the law or an absolute requirement that all instances of lawbreaking be punished, then the case against extending amnesty would be conclusive apart from any considerations that might be pressed in its favor. What I argue in this chapter is that such a definitive or conclusive case cannot be made. The first section contains responses to the most common objections to setting aside the punishment of war resisters, especially those created by the Vietnam war, by contending that there are other values more important than retribution, deterrence, or even law. The argument in the second part is carried on at a somewhat more abstract level, dealing with more technical philosophical objections to amnesty. The thesis in both sections is that politics and law are two alternative ways of reconciling the conflicts between men and that, finally, politics is more important than law.

A Matter of Punishment

Among the first set of reasons for rejecting amnesty, three points recur. Failure to prosecute those who refuse to participate in a war is an affront to the families and friends of those killed or wounded in the war; amnesty, in this view, would "dishonor" those who served in Vietnam. Draft evaders and resisters increase the risk of military service for others by reducing the manpower pool of potential conscripts; military deserters endanger the lives of other soldiers and violate their oath of service. Granting an amnesty after any war would encourage resistance and desertion in future wars, when conscription again may be needed, by setting the harmful precedent of forgetting and forgiving such acts.

Each of these statements is descriptive and prescriptive. That is, each describes or predicts certain actions in such a way that the conclusion that those actions ought to be punished seems unavoidable. Each proposition is an attempt to justify the punishment of war resisters.

Few persons hold the harsh position that we should punish political offenders simply to "get even." That sounds too much like vengeance—the notion that punishment itself is a good. The only protection against increasing suffering needlessly is to insist that any increase in the amount of suffering result in some benefit to other persons or to society.[1]

From this perspective, the belief that amnesty is an affront to those who lost a son, husband, or friend in a war is the most dismaying complaint against amnesty. As James Reston, Jr., has argued, this complaint pits victims against victims—those who suffer in a war and those who suffer exile.[2] Nothing done to war resisters can repair the direct personal losses that many suffer during a war. It is conceivable that punishment of war resisters might provide some with psychological comfort. But a national policy that attempts to comfort grief by creating more grief adds another cost to the price of a war. In the case of a

1. See Ted Honderich, *Punishment: The Supposed Justifications* (Baltimore, 1971), p. 49. I have relied heavily upon this small but thoughtful book in my replies to the claims made for punishment by the critics of amnesty. More technical but also helpful is Stanley E. Grupp, ed., *Theories of Punishment* (Bloomington, Ind., 1972).

2. In *Selective Service and Amnesty*, p. 654.

war such as the one in Vietnam, sentencing war resisters to prison or the exiles to a lifetime of separation from their families and friends would only prolong the memories of America's most divisive foreign war. As in every war, the present and future have more claim to our attention than the past. It was Aristotle who advised that "the past and present are necessary, the future is possible."

Amnesty is an acknowledgment of the convictions of those who refuse to serve, at least to the extent of recognizing the doubts and controversy surrounding a particular war. If there is reasonable doubt about a war, a sensible response is to set aside the punishment of those who are the first to believe what others only later come to question. Although they are unlikely to recognize it, even those who serve in a war have an interest in providing some alternative for those caught in the situation of fighting in a war they consider unjust or going to jail. Every man is a potential civil disobedient. Those who serve are quite justified in feeling that the burden of service should be shared equally. What is at issue is the question of whether or not fairness is compromised by amnesty. If, in imagining himself in the position of those who feel they cannot participate in a war such as Vietnam, the reluctant conscript would want some alternative to punishment available for himself, then I do not think fairness is compromised by amnesty. By surrounding himself with a "veil of ignorance" so as to avoid knowing how amnesty would affect his own case, the individual is better able to limit his response to general rather than personal considerations.[3] Perhaps no one can truly become the impartial spectator or judge hypothesized by many moral philosophers, but amnesty must be considered from the side of both those who fight and those who refuse to fight—from the standpoint of the family that loses a son in the war and the family whose son is in exile—without knowing, however, to which side or which family one belongs.

Looking at the second objection to amnesty, the rationale for punishing draft resisters and deserters is that they unlawfully avoid certain duties that they equally share with others. Justice or impartiality demands that persons with the same responsi-

3. The concepts of a "veil of ignorance" and the impartial spectator are developed by John Rawls, A Theory of Justice (Cambridge, 1971), pp. 136–42.

bilities be treated similarly if they respond equally to their duties, but those who fail to respond must be punished in order
for justice to be meaningful. Punishment, then, is the fitting
dessert for the resister's action. Nothing more is needed to justify his punishment than his past behavior. Punishment is retribution for that behavior.

Admittedly, deserters and draft evaders do increase other
men's odds for service under a system of conscription, but the
statistical increase is very small when the manpower pool is
large. Nor was there, to my knowledge, a single case of desertion during the Vietnam war that directly exposed others to
greater danger. Most deserters were soldiers stationed at either
American bases or American installations in Europe, who fled
upon receiving orders to Vietnam. The deserters within Vietnam typically fled when off duty. Nevertheless, it is clear that
such men refuse a service that others perform. The point of amnesty is to admit, however, that such refusal, in the case of Vietnam, was understandable and can be tolerated. Of course, amnesty means treating some men differently from other men; the
case for amnesty is an argument for just such *differential*
treatment.

Every religious conscientious objector also reduces the size
of the manpower pool; every student deferment during the Vietnam war increased the odds that another would be drafted.[4]
In recognizing the consciences of religious objectors or in
granting student deferments, the government and public treat
them differently from others. All such acts of discrimination
obviously involve a judgment that in this case there are good
reasons for setting aside the rule of impartiality. Just as there
are good reasons for exempting religious conscientious objectors from service, there may be compelling reasons at times for
an amnesty that exempts the selective conscientious objector

4. The claim that the American exiles increased other men's odds for service
is true but misleading insofar as critics pretend that all eligible males were
equally vulnerable to the chance of military service. In 1968, of 20,829,000 draft
registrants aged 18½ to 26, some 2.2 million had student deferments, 4,126,000
were deferred on the basis of fatherhood or hardship, 471,000 had occupational
or agricultural deferments, and some 424,000 were unclassified: *Statistical Abstract of the United States,* 90th ed. (Washington, 1969), p. 260, Table 383; cited
by David Malament, "Selective Conscientious Objection and the *Gillette* Decision," *Philosophy and Public Affairs* 1 (Summer 1972):381–82.

from punishment. The ideal of impartiality built into the rule of law does not prohibit us from ever calculating the unusual case. Nor, as a special measure, does amnesty threaten the generality of the rule of law. Since amnesty, as a law, excuses a past offense, it in no way grants permission to break the law in the future. Amnesty is an after-the-fact legal recognition of the refusal of a quite specific military service. What amnesty does deny is that there is an iron link between lawbreaking and punishment.

Granting this much of the argument, a critic of amnesty still might warn that a government that excuses or overlooks the offenses of some runs the risk of arbitrariness in the future with all of the attendant dangers for unfairness toward others in the political community. The statement that "justice is blind" nicely captures the legalist conception of a just society. It means that men ought to be treated equally before the law regardless of their race, class, or income, and that those who break the law ought to be punished out of fairness to those who obey the law. The central fallacy behind this argument is that, first, it treats law as something separated from the surrounding social context. Second, it treats the values surrounding law as exclusive values.[5]

Partiality, in contrast to the legalist conception, is on many occasions preferable to impartiality. Cities, for example, have found no difficulty in setting aside the letter of the law that prohibits strikes by public employees so as to arrive at an agreement whereby trash can be collected again, fires fought, or streets patrolled. Nor is there anything wrong with such behavior unless one assumes that enforcing the law is always the only value worth looking after. In a morally pluralistic world, it is often more important that several different values be permitted to live together in compromise, even though logically one might exclude another. Where two goods such as the impartial enforcement of the law and the partiality of setting aside punishment for the sake of reconciliation compete, there is no iron law that dictates that the values of law must always override other values. Even when punishment is permitted by the fact that a law has been broken, considerations of kindness,

5. Cf. Shklar, *Legalism*, pp. 104–7, 121–22.

doubts about the immorality of the illegal action, a desire for unity, and many other things can easily justify the decision not to implement the punishment. It does not follow from the fact that a law has been broken that we are under an obligation to punish the lawbreaker. Men have the capacity to reason precisely to protect themselves from the straitjacket of their own rules.

The politics behind a law is easy to see whenever a city does not prosecute a strong policemen's union for engaging in a work stoppage. The strength of the union and the importance of the policemen's services to the community justify the prudent decision to reach an accommodation rather than to insist upon punishment. Similarly, once the majority of the American public recognized the questionable nature of the Vietnam war, it was no longer fitting to punish political offenders for breaking the law that served that war policy.[6] Political judgments should at times override legal rules.[7]

Selective Service Director Curtis W. Tarr reflected the third objection to amnesty, when he testified before a Senate hearing, that if a post-Vietnam amnesty made it possible for those who avoided the draft "to return to the full rights of citizenship without any penalty, then it would be difficult to justify the continuation of inductions."[8] While the adoption of the all-volunteer army has made this particular point moot, the issue of amnesty's fairness to those who did respond to the draft during the Vietnam war remains. There is also the broader but

6. Technically, whether or not a majority recognizes the doubtful morality of a policy cannot be determinate in deciding when a policy is moral or immoral. It is not right to punish even the single individual who stands against every other man if his stand is the right one. Numbers do not make morality. Practically, numbers do matter, and it becomes all the more unjust to punish men when their convictions are held as serious doubts by the majority. It also makes less sense to punish them when they are, in effect, a significant minority community within the larger democratic community.

7. A great deal about the difference between "politics" and "crime" can be learned from the essay by Harry R. Blaine and David Kettler, "Law as a Political Weapon," *Politics and Society* 1 (August 1971):479–526. Blaine and Kettler's argument that much of the student protest at Ohio State University involved an alternative interpretation of the function of the university and that their protest was thus political rather than simply criminal parallels part of my case for amnesty. The illegality of the exiles' actions must not obscure the political considerations behind those actions.

8. *Selective Service and Amnesty*, p. 46.

more ambiguous question of whether amnesty would encourage desertion and other forms of resistance in future wars. There always remains the possibility that the country will again decide to resort to conscription. Discussion of Tarr's statement can be helpful, then, insofar as it reveals the dilemma that conscription creates for a war's opponents.

The use of conscription for any war raises a host of philosophical and political problems. It is far from clear that the individual ever has an obligation to die for the state, except possibly in cases of national defense where the preservation of the individual and the preservation of the state coincide. Various of the social contract writers contend that consenting to be a member of a political order entails the obligation of military service if the state demands it. There are, however, all sorts of difficulties surrounding the definition of consent to a political system. Michael Walzer fairly argues that if consent includes the duty to die for the state, consent should be more meaningful than mere residency or the accident of being born in a particular country at a particular time.[9] Birth alone hardly is sufficient to produce the feeling that one has an obligation to risk life itself for the state.

To meet such problems, most writers attach to the idea of consent such requirements as the opportunity to participate meaningfully in the politics of the community over a period of time.[10] Such participation or its availability might be taken by the state and other citizens as a sign that one is a consenting member of the society. But even by these fairly loose tests, most draftees during the Vietnam war had little if any opportunity to participate in the decisions of their government. If men must do something to acquire an obligation, it is difficult to say that these men had a duty to serve in the military.

Perhaps all of this suggests that the most compelling reason for doing away with conscription is that it places the individual in an intolerable dilemma. It leaves the individual experiencing conflicting obligations or loyalties—to the democratic state but not to the Vietnam war—with the alternatives of exile, imprisonment, or fighting in a war that he considers unjust, to reconcile

9. *Obligations*, chaps. 4–5, passim.
10. Cf. Robert Booth Fowler, "Political Obligation and the Draft," in Hanson and Fowler, *Obligation and Dissent*, pp. 46–62.

these diverse feelings. A democratic state, it cannot be argued often enough, will always attempt to reduce the number of situations where the citizen faces such harsh choices. Adoption of the all-volunteer army is a major step toward the awareness that however important loyalty to the state ranks it is not an exclusive loyalty.

These and related topics, however, threaten to take us too far afield from Tarr's testimony. With Tarr's statement, the brief against amnesty moved from the past to the future, from retribution to deterrence. Does an amnesty make future war resistance more likely? This question cannot be answered yes or no. But previous amnesties have not had the effect of hampering later war efforts. (I think this objection is a case of partisans to a political issue exaggerating the attention that later generations are likely to pay to what they do.) The policy of no longer sending draftees to Vietnam was accompanied by a large drop in the number of draft resistance and desertion cases.

Some still will insist that amnesty might make future resistance more likely. Of course it might. If the United States decided to pursue another war like Vietnam or to send large numbers of soldiers into some other part of Indochina, amnesty might encourage resistance later. But resistance in such instances is likely regardless of whether amnesty is granted or withheld. Punishment provides little hope for discouraging war resisters. We know that the severe penalties imposed for violations of the Selective Service Act during World War II had no discernible effect in persuading men to comply with the law. Courts that were strict in imposing penalties had as many cases before them as lenient courts.[11] The harsh penalties given the earliest draft resisters during the Vietnam war did not stem the rise of evasion. Aside from another Vietnam, amnesty might just as easily have no effect upon support for future government policies.

What opponents of amnesty are asking us to do is to treat the abstract *possibility* that amnesty *might* encourage future resistance as though it were already an established fact and then to use this "fact" as a reason for opposing amnesty.[12] But in calculating the consequences of amnesty, as of any policy, remote

11. Sibley and Jacob, *Conscription of Conscience*, p. 476.
12. Quade, "Selective Conscientious Objection," p. 349.

possibilities and fears must give way to immediate benefits where these can be had for no cost. It is as great an error to look to the abstract future as to the agonies of the past in trying to find our way toward reconciliation among citizens.

LEGALISM

Let us recall where we are. Up to this point, discussion has been about the most popular, that is, widespread, objections to amnesty. These objections, I have contended, are not conclusive in that they do not rule out setting aside punishment for political offenses. But these objections can be strengthened in a number of ways. There is a set of more strictly philosophical commentaries on the rule of law and disobedience that argues that in the interest of the former the latter must always be punished. And although the Vietnam war resisters did not commit civil disobedience in the traditional sense—they did not act publicly, they did not accept the legal consequences of their actions, points taken up in the next chapter—they did by their actions affirm that other values were more important to them than law-abidingness. It is this characteristic that their disobedience shares with more familiar forms of civil disobedience. Not surprisingly, writers who have strong reservations about civil disobedience are either explicitly opposed to any amnesty or their writings would logically lead them to this position.

In a contribution to a collection of essays on amnesty and in his recent book *Political Violence and Civil Disobedience*, the social philosopher Ernest van den Haag nicely outlines the political posture that I have called legalism.[13] Positively, legalism asserts rule of law, as long as there is an operating democracy, as its highest moral principle. Negatively, legalism denies that there is ever a "right" to disobey the law, since it defines moral behavior as a matter of legal rule-following. The major consequence of legalism that will concern me is its tendency to translate all political disputes and conflicts into questions of legal right and wrong. By translating the political question of draft

13. For van den Haag's comments on amnesty, see his contribution to Murray Polner, ed., *When Can I Come Home?* (New York, 1972), pp. 142–49, and the exchange of letters with this writer in *Dissent* (Summer 1974), pp. 461–63. For his views on civil disobedience, see *Political Violence and Civil Disobedience* (New York, 1972).

resistance and desertion into a judicial question, the legalist attempts to define the type of problem that we are required to
deal with in such a way that punishment—the judicial solution
to legal wrongdoing—appears as the most logical solution. Much
can be said for the legalist's mansion but not nearly as much
as the legalist imagines.

At the center of van den Haag's insistence upon the priority
of law-abidingness is the recognition that a democracy must
find some method for making decisions. Until the arrival of an-
archic bliss, unanimity is impossible. Indeed, unanimity would
be intolerable and oppressive. If we had to wait until every-
one agreed that a problem needs solving, a group needs help,
a minority requires protection, or a bridge needs repairing,
chaos and suffering would result. Just as a government makes
policies in these areas, so war is a policy that nations sometimes adopt; to have any policy, including the decision to go to
war, would seem to require that the minority give way to the
majority. In other words, politically counting men as equals,
democracy still needs some machinery for translating popular
sovereignty into a method of decision-making. Majority rule
whereby the decision of a majority of the lawmakers who have
in turn been elected by a majority of the public binds the entire
public is this translation mechanism. What offends van den
Haag about disobedience to the law is that it thwarts majority
rule by giving a veto power to a minority. Disobedience, he
argues, is an attack upon democracy. "In a democracy," he
writes, ". . . what I am doing by not obeying the law is defying
the majority in favor of a minority view. And I am not in favor
of a minority dictatorship."[14]

With this objection, van den Haag falls into a pit of pernicious abstractions. He mistakenly equates disobedience to a
particular law or defiance of a specific policy with dictatorial
rule of the few over the many. One doubts that he would call
a country governed by a military clique a democracy if that
clique on one occasion abided by the outcome of a national
referendum. Van den Haag's argument also depends upon the
refusal to recognize the differences between rebels and revolutionaries.[15] Revolutionaries do indeed seek the total transfor-

14. In Polner, p. 148.
15. This confusion is evident, in my opinion, in van den Haag's concept of

mation of the state. But what evidence is there to support the view that the exiles of the Vietnam era were fighting for such a goal? The exiles were rebels—individuals who defied the government's war policy. One cannot equate this defiance with an attack upon democracy or the larger framework of rule of law.

Van den Haag's case rests upon the assumption either that all laws are good laws or that law-abidingness will always be less harmful than any form of disobedience, however limited. These assumptions are impossible to maintain. Segregation laws are not moral simply because they are the law. And defiance of those laws has done more to further democracy than compliance ever could have done. The exiles pressed a similar case against the laws supporting the Vietnam war. That case cannot be dismissed merely by hyperbole that warns of minority dictatorship.

Meriting more serious consideration is the contention that amnesty is, in effect, a policy that sanctions selective conscientious objection. Opponents of a particular war, it is argued, pose a greater threat to the state's authority and the principles necessary for the rule of law to work than universal conscientious objectors. Van den Haag represents this position when he writes, "it is one thing to renounce war as a means to anything, another to spurn only a particular war—just as it is one thing to repudiate the death penalty in principle, and another to oppose inflicting it on a particular defendant. Motivation may well be moral in both instances. But the conscience which only objects to some wars or death sentences depends on judgments of specific facts; whereas the conscience opposed, in principle, to all wars, regardless of circumstances, or to the death penalty, does not. The objector's judgment of specific facts (is *this* defendant actually guilty? Is *this* war necessary, useful, or just?) could not be allowed to prevail over that of courts and governments, without reducing their judgments to an opinion no more authoritative and enforceable than his."[16] I do not want to underestimate the forcefulness of this argument. It is one that

---

"coercive civil disobedience," which is equivalent to violent revolution. By placing the adjective *coercive* in front of civil disobedience, van den Haag confuses the civil disobedient's resistance to a particular law and the revolutionary's effort to overthrow the entire legal order. See *Political Violence and Civil Disobedience*, pp. 29–30.

16. Ibid., p. 5.

the Supreme Court has often endorsed in rejecting the claims
of selective conscientious objectors. In one of many cases
coming out of the Vietnam war, the Court upheld the conviction of a conscientious objector not because it doubted the sincerity of his objection to military service, "but because [his]
objection ran to a particular war."[17] In support of its conclusion, the Court reasoned that any exemption from military service was a matter of legislative grace and not a right guaranteed
by the Constitution. Further, the Court argued that Congress has
the right to determine whether selective conscientious objection threatens other legitimate government interests, such as
the need to maintain an effective national defense. While ac-
knowledging the desirability of avoiding the coercion of conscience, the Court reasoned that this value must be weighed
against other goods important to the political community.

Critics of the Court's decisions on selective conscientious objection have responded in a variety of ways. Locating how my
criticism differs from some of these more familiar responses
should sharpen the reasoning behind my defense of amnesty.
Briefly, most critics of the Court first complain that exempting
the universal but not the selective objector from military service effects an arbitrary and unconstitutional discrimination. But
I know of no adequate response to the Court's argument that
exemption from military service is an act of legislative grace
rather than a right guaranteed by the First Amendment's "free
exercise of religion" clause. As long as war is recognized as a
legitimate policy that a people might adopt in the interest of
national security, then some "body" must decide when to adopt
that policy. And the very meaning of democratic politics or, indeed, politics of any sort is that a collective decision must override the particular preferences of individuals.

A second and more philosophical complaint made by those
who favor selective conscientious objection is that conscience
should never be coerced. In this view, "selective objection
would be a natural extension of our present recognition of the
rights of the [universal] conscientious objector."[18] But this
position similarly errs in imagining that conscience, whatever
its moral standing, can be treated as an absolute political good.

17. United States v. Gillette, 401 U.S. 437 (1971), cited by Malament, p. 364.
18. Roger L. Shinn, *Christianity and Crisis* (April 17, 1967), pp. 73–74.

If conscience is an absolute value, then the only appeal left when my conscience clashes with your conscience is either to some form of force or to the state. In Gordon Schochet's words, "my conscience and my moral commitments are entirely too personal to provide a basis—let alone a justification—for your behavior. . . . By appealing to conscience I am running the risk of eliminating further discussion. Having put the matter in these terms, there is very little I can say to you if your moral intuitions do not correspond to mine."[19] In the last resort, Hobbes is probably correct in calling clubs trumps. But the rule of law is intended to prevent us from reaching the last resort.

The weakness behind the case for selective conscientious objection is that its supporters have not "reconciled themselves to a political framework for thinking and speaking on political matters."[20] Politics can reconcile two absolute and abstract goods in a way that logic cannot. On one side, there is the desire to permit the individual to refuse participation in a policy that he cannot support in good faith. But opposed to this good is the equally strong desire to maintain the authority of the state. As long as the issue is framed as a choice between the absolute value of conscience and the absolute good of authority, no reconciliation of the two values is possible. But what evidence is there for the proposition that we were, once the Vietnam war ended, in fact confronted with such a Hobbesian dilemma? Why not, as Quentin L. Quade has persuasively argued, replace apocalyptic questions about conscience and authority with the more political question of the likely consequences of following one course of action or another?

If it is indeed possible to reconstruct the amnesty argument around this more pragmatic basis, then van den Haag is guilty of the same error as the advocates of selective conscientious objection. Neither side sees issues such as exemption from service and amnesty as practical questions about what, on balance, should be done in a given situation. While van den Haag is correct in holding that, in the abstract, the government's opinion must take precedence over the selective objector's opinion,

19. "From Dissent to Disobedience: A Justification of Rational Protest," *Politics and Society* 1 (February 1971):246–47. Also cf. his "Morality of Resisting the Penalty," in Virginia Held, Kai Nielson, and Charles Parsons, eds., *Philosophy and Political Action* (New York, 1972), pp. 175–96.

20. Quade, p. 343.

it is the very abstractness of his contention that is unsatisfactory. As I have argued elsewhere,[21] what this position cannot show is whether in any particular situation we are in fact faced with endorsing one value, the respect for conscience, at the expense of another, the state's authority. In the case of Vietnam, once the war was over, conscription abolished, and illegal political resistance ended, there was little risk to the norm of obedience in a decision to grant amnesty. The greater risk is the attitude that makes state authority a good that must always supersede all others. Rather than a logical juxtaposition of abstract values, what is needed is a political judgment about the costs and benefits of amnesty in a specific situation.

I confess that my discussion of the issue of selective conscientious objection was, in part, a detour, one that I judged worth making so as to clarify my thesis that it is possible to favor amnesty in particular without arguing for selective conscientious objection in general. The arguments against the latter, which I find persuasive, simply do not touch the case for amnesty. Legalism and moralism advocate different final goods, but both assume what politics attempts to discover—the appropriate and shifting priority among values in a world where no fixed hierarchy of ends is possible. Rather than equating justice with law or, conversely, the right to disobey, justice must be seen as a balancing of men's competing obligations. Equating law with justice encourages the harmful illusion that indiscriminate obedience to the law insures a just order. Equating the right to disobey with justice blinds us to Hobbes' warning that where every man is a law unto himself justice has no place.

The legalist, who now interests me more than the moralist, can fall back upon different ground to buttress his weakening position. Granting that specific acts of disobedience do not forebode catastrophe for the rule of law, the legalist can still deny that the individual has a "right" to oppose the majority by illegal means and that if he does so he must accept his punishment. The political theorist Harry Jaffa puts it this way: "To abide by majority rule does not mean resigning our consciences. It means rather that we have, as citizens, surrendered our natural freedom to act independently, in order that we may have the cooperation of other men who have equally surrendered

21. See my "In Defense of Amnesty," *Dissent* (Winter 1974):90–94.

their natural freedom to act independently. We have made a bargain with others, and as honest men we have a duty to keep that bargain—so long, at least, as good faith is kept with us."[22] As a general observation about fidelity to law and orderliness in society, this statement invites acceptance. Each individual does benefit considerably from the general law-abidingness of others. They, in turn, have every reason to expect him to obey the laws for their sake. Reciprocity, whether in respect for others' rights or common support of the law, is a critical part of what is meant by the teaching that men are political equals. The law helps men to predict each other's behavior by narrowing the area of random actions. It is thus an important source of that trust among men which makes the benefits of cooperation possible. Within the framework of a shared legal system, no two men are complete strangers; each already knows a great deal of what to expect from the other. From this perspective, it is argued that the individual who deserts or avoids the draft does more than commit a technical offense. Rather, he violates his moral covenant with other citizens. By punishing defiance of the law, the state encourages men to keep their bargain and thereby reaffirms the importance of trust and cooperation in men's affairs.

I have no quarrel with Professor Jaffa's defense of the contribution that a system of law can make to social trust and harmony. Nor would I object to the contention that men are under an obligation to keep faith with each other. But this social-contract model of law argues something much more difficult to maintain. The contention is that there is never a moral right to defy the law in a democracy, since the individual breaks his promise by defying a law that has been passed by democratic procedures.

Between the premise—men have formed a social pact—and the conclusion—breaking the law is immoral—three major difficulties intervene. First, there is the question of what constitutes a sign that an individual has been made a partner in the democratic lawmaking procedures. At the minimum, I argued earlier that one wants to say that where individuals have not had any

22. "Reflections on Thoreau and Lincoln: Civil Disobedience and the American Tradition," in Robert A. Goldwin, ed., On Civil Disobedience (Chicago, 1968), p. 38 (my emphasis).

meaningful chance to take part in the political affairs of their government, they are not yet part of the social compact. Disaffected groups—whether blacks denied access to the political system, the poor without the resources of time, knowledge, and influence to have a share in the public's business, or the alienated youth dismayed by policies such as Vietnam made long before many of them reached political maturity—stand outside of the social compact. No one has struck a bargain with them. Second, the model oversimplifies and distorts the reality of men's obligations or promises. Loyalty to the state exists among a multitude of loyalties. The obligation to obey the law must compete with loyalties to family, friends, and even class. Nor do these competing loyalties derive merely from interpersonal relations with others. We are quite accustomed to speaking of a man who is faithful to a cause, his beliefs, or a political program opposed to the government's. The proposition that men are bound as honest men to keep their bargains is not by itself sufficient to dictate which bargain, promise, or commitment must be honored.

Even if these objections could be met, there remains a third difficulty with Jaffa's argument that most clearly applies to the circumstances of war resisters of the Vietnam era. Recalling the social contract argument, it makes obedience to the law conditional upon faith being kept with the citizens. But we had numerous examples pointing to a government pattern of bad faith.[23] The publication of the Pentagon Papers revealed the efforts of various administrations to cover up and distort the

---

23. In this connection, one must cite *The Pentagon Papers*, which reveal at least three types of systematic deception by various administrations. Beginning with President Eisenhower, the American government authorized various secret military raids headed by the Central Intelligence Agency within Vietnam, in direct opposition to the announced support of the Geneva agreements. A second major form of deception was to ask the American public for support *after* a set of commitments had been made or some action taken. Thus, Kennedy introduced military forces into Vietnam under the guise of flood relief assistance. Subsequently, the American public was asked to support its men serving in Vietnam. Finally, Lyndon Johnson perfected the art of half-truths whereby the public was told that the United States sought no wider war, which was true but irrelevant since the government had concluded that it was being "forced" into a wider war, a point kept from the public. On the manipulation of Congressional opinion, see John Galloway, *The Gulf of Tonkin Resolution* (Rutherford, N.J., 1970); a later Congress withdrew this resolution, convinced that the earlier Congress had been deceived.

origins and nature of American fighting in Vietnam. Whenever the national government lies to the public, attempts to manipulate the news, and vigorously discourages dissent at home, it is the government, not the exiles, that has broken faith with the conditions necessary for the democratic rule of law to work.

It is this deception by the government that is most directly relevant to the issue of whether or not the American exiles violated their obligations to the state in refusing military service. Obligations cannot exist in an atmosphere of bad faith and lying in politics. Charges of bad faith against the exiles or that they turned their backs upon America are simply wide of the mark. The government turned its back upon its own citizens, and this is only one more factor supporting the exiles' belief that the government's claim upon their service was illegitimate and justly rejected.

AMNESTY AND OPEN POLITICS

The legal language of crime and punishment obscures the far more important political issue of responsible and irresponsible government power. Government policies in a democracy are only authoritative when they are made by leaders subject to public pressure. Policies must be made within an order characterized by openness, that is, the opportunity for citizen influence upon the policy makers. This does not mean that every policy must be every citizen's policy; political participation does not guarantee that one will always win. What political openness does insure is that public influence will be one of the chief factors that will enter into the calculations of leaders choosing a course of action that commits the resources and even the lives of the public. Setting aside the punishment of those forced into exile or imprisoned by their opposition to a policy evolved in deceit can be a step toward a public and official renewal of the commitment to the politics of openness and a step away from the closed politics of manipulation and propaganda.

5. The Case for Amnesty

In the mixed society of coercion and nature,
our characteristic act is Drawing the Line,
beyond which we cannot co-operate. All
the heart-searching and purgatorial anxiety
concerns this question, Where to draw the
line? . . . Well! there is a boyish joke I
like to tell. Tom says to Jerry: "Do you
want to fight? Cross that line!" and Jerry
does. "Now," cries Tom, "you're on my side!"

We draw the line in their conditions; we
proceed on our conditions.
                Paul Goodman, *Drawing the Line*

ORDINARY politics means such things as lobbying, campaigning, and voting. But at times the political stakes are raised and divisions of opinion give rise to extraordinary political actions involving disobedience to the law or political offenses. Two types of extraordinary political protests are widely accepted today—breaking the law to test its constitutionality, and defiance of the law even after it has been ruled constitutional, as long as the disobedient accepts the legal consequences of his actions. The Vietnam war produced a new type of extraordinary political opposition. By refusing to accept imprisonment for their disobedience, the exiles went beyond traditional forms of civil disobedience and conscientious refusal. Also, they were as concerned about the political and moral failures of the war as its legal or constitutional faults. That is, their protest was against a political or policy decision of their government rather than against a particular law. While some of the war's opponents did challenge the constitutionality of the war, the exiles sought to evade a policy rather than to bring a court test of some law. But whatever specific form disobedience assumes—resistance, evasion, desertion—it is an assertion by an individual that at this point he must draw the line between what the state demands and what he can accept. His act of refusal sets him against other men; but that same act, if it affirms important values, lays the groundwork for a new unity in which those values are more secure. This chapter begins with a review of extraordinary political actions and the types of considerations that justify drawing the line. It ends in a defense of the values affirmed by the exiles' actions.

Political offenses are criminal acts, but they can easily be distinguished from nonpolitical criminal acts. A burglar, for example, steals for private gain, but the legendary Robin Hood who robbed the rich to aid the poor was not only a criminal but also a political rebel. The person who falsifies his income tax statement so as to increase his wealth commits a nonpolitical crime. In contrast, the man who announces his intention not to pay his federal income tax as a protest against a war is a political offender. A pacifist who refuses to comply with an induction notice is similarly a political actor. What sets off political offenses from other offenses is that the law is broken not merely to seek personal advantage but either to change the law or, less optimistically, to refuse participation in a policy of questionable constitutionality, morality, or simple wisdom. Political offenses are direct challenges to the government's authority. In nonpolitical crimes against private persons or property the government exercises its police power to protect one person from another; political contests find the government itself as the party against whom the offense is committed.

At their most dramatic, political offenses include such acts as treason, rebellion, assassination, and mutiny. Governments can also be guilty of political crimes such as violations of civil rights, bribery, vote fraud, and any other act that undermines the basic principles of the political order. Since the exiles created by the Vietnam war did not commit violent acts, discussion here is limited to nonviolent disobedience of the law—draft resistance, desertion, and peaceful but illegal protest against the Vietnam war. Considering the justification of these acts will involve, in turn, charges that the government was guilty of such political offenses as waging an unconstitutional war and violating the rules of war. The comments throughout are, of course, limited to a society that aspires to achieve the ideals of a democratic community.

What intensifies the conflict between the government and its opponents during an extraordinary political contest is that each side charges the other with committing politically criminal acts. A resister defies a law because he believes that it is unconstitutional or immoral. The government, he charges, is the wrongdoer. The government, on the other hand, insists upon obedience to the law as an affirmation of its own legitimacy. Even when the Supreme Court rules on the constitutional issue, there is no guarantee that the struggle will end. The government, if the ruling goes against it, may be lax in enforcing the new law of the land. If the ruling goes against the citizen, he may continue his defiance on the basis that the Court has erred.

No government can tolerate violent resistance to its laws or policies. The state's monopoly of coercive force is too central to the existence and integrity of the state to make room for the private use of violence. But there are at least two forms of non-violent political disobedience that the democratic state can accommodate—civil disobedience and conscientious refusal. By accommodation, I mean a decision not to prosecute such defiance of the law. A violation of the law, it will be recalled, is a necessary condition permitting the government to punish someone, but it does not follow that the government must exercise this permission. All sorts of other values may lead to the judgment that setting aside prosecution is the wiser and fairer course. There are a number of familiar, albeit rather insignificant, examples that illustrate this point. A city decides to take no action against a large crowd celebrating a football victory even though it is blocking traffic in violation of a city ordinance. A city does not invoke the laws against marijuana smoking for a crowd at a rock concert. In either case, the judgment is the same. Public tranquility is best served by not attempting to punish violations of the law. To always insist that "the law is the law" is to fly into a realm of abstraction completely divorced from the realities of human situations.[1]

---

1. The rule-of-law model also conflicts with the realities of the legal system. The model argues that there can never be a legitimate, i.e., legal, departure from the requirement to follow the law. But, in fact, the legal system sanctions several types of legitimate rule departures. Juries, for example, have the discretionary power to deliver a verdict contrary to the law if they judge that there are other more important considerations, and the legal system indirectly acknowledges this power in that there is no method for holding the jurors to account or

Normally, the decision not to prosecute is an informal one; simply no action is taken by the government. But amnesty is a legal measure that enables the government to nullify officially the penalties attached to some law. Since governments are always imbued with the values of legalism, one of the merits of amnesty is that it is a legal measure for dealing with the legalist's value of law enforcement. The law can be both honored and set aside.

The fact that the state can tolerate certain instances of disobedience does not solve the problem of when it should be tolerant. Some argue that it must never tolerate lawbreaking. If one person or group, it is argued, is permitted to defy the law, there is nothing to prevent other groups from defying laws that displease them. This is the domestic version of the domino theory. Just as the fall of one government is supposed to lead to the toppling of other governments, so specific acts of disobedience supposedly lead to general disobedience.

The practical response to such reasoning is that there is as much difficulty in finding evidence to support a domestic domino theory as there is for one in international relations. If it were true that disobedience in one case encourages disobedience in many more cases, there should be no difficulty in documenting such experiences. Howard Zinn has fairly argued that if these fears were true, "we might expect either that persons engaging in civil disobedience become general law violators, or that other persons are encouraged by these acts to become indiscriminate violators of law. There is no indication that this has happened. For instance, Negroes in the south who began to violate segregation laws in organized campaigns of civil disobedience did not at the same time become general lawbreakers, nor did this lead to a larger crime rate among others in the population. Indeed, it was found in Albany, Georgia, that during the mass demonstrations and the mass disobedience there in 1961 and 1962, the general crime rate declined."[2]

There is, however, more involved here than just the domino

---

any way to punish them. Similarly, prosecutors are largely immune from punishment when they exercise their discretion to decide when and whom to indict or whether to indict at all. For a systematic treatment of these and other legal departures from the letter of the law, see Mortimer R. Kadish and Sanford H. Kadish, *Discretion to Disobey* (Stanford, 1973).

2. *Disobedience and Democracy* (New York, 1968), pp. 12–13.

theory. Even if it could be proven that the failure to punish a bank robber does not lead to a rise in the number of bank robberies, no one would advocate freeing all bank robbers. In addition to distinguishing political offenses from ordinary crimes, a distinction must be made between principled and nonprincipled resistance. Such a distinction will carry us some way in showing that just because one favors some forms of disobedience, it does not follow that he is committed to favoring any form of disobedience. One might, for example, approve a religious community's disobedience of a law requiring it to send its children to a public school, disobedience that has now been ruled constitutional by the Supreme Court. But approval of this disobedience might very easily be accompanied by disapproval of a religious group's disobedience of a law requiring children to be inoculated against a polio epidemic. It is a theory in support of discriminate disobedience rather than indiscriminate disobedience that is needed.

Once we possess a theory of principled disobedience, there still remains the task of deciding whether or not the disobedients' principles or convictions are capable of becoming *our* principles or convictions. A segregationist might well disobey civil rights laws out of a sincere and principled conviction that they are harmful to a traditional way of life. At this point, the substantive evaluation of what it is that the segregationist values must replace the discussion of whether or not his disobedience meets the procedural criteria of principled resistance. That is why it is necessary to talk about the origin, constitutionality, and prosecution of the Vietnam war. It is not enough to show that the exiles were sincere in their opposition; sincerity as an issue must be replaced or, more exactly, complemented by the issue of the war.

CIVIL DISOBEDIENCE AND CONSCIENTIOUS REFUSAL

One of the most widely held definitions of civil disobedience is that offered by Hugo A. Bedau: "Any one commits an act of civil disobedience if and only if he acts illegally, publicly, nonviolently, and conscientiously with the intent to frustrate [one of] the laws, policies, or decisions of his government."[3] The

3. "On Civil Disobedience," *Journal of Philosophy* 58 (October 12, 1961):661.

illegality of the action is what most obviously separates civil disobedience from ordinary politics. For a long time the prevailing view has restricted justifiable disobedience to acts aimed at testing the constitutionality of some law. If the court agrees with the challenge, the citizen is said, retrospectively, not to have acted illegally. But if the court rejects his challenge, the citizen is then expected to accept the legal judgment, even though he may still hold the moral judgment that the law is wrong. This teaching on civil disobedience has been given new currency by a former justice of the Supreme Court, Abe Fortas, who writes in a short book, "The motive of civil disobedience, whatever its type, does not confer immunity for law violation. . . . If he is properly arrested, charged, and convicted, he should be punished by fine or imprisonment, or both, in accordance with the provisions of the law, unless the law is invalid in general or as applied. He may be motivated by the highest moral principles. He may be passionately inspired. He may, indeed, be right in the eyes of history or morality or philosophy. These are not controlling. It is the state's duty to arrest and punish those who violate the laws designed to protect private safety and public order."[4] Fortas, a legalist, makes many of the errors of legalism in this short paragraph. He assumes throughout his essay that "safety" and "order" as defined by the government are always preferable to the values represented by illegal protest. He neglects the distinction between the permission to punish an offense and the issue of whether or not it is desirable to exercise that permission. His teaching excludes conscientious refusal that aims not as much at testing the constitutionality of some law as at refusing to participate in an unjust policy, however acceptable the legal processes by which it is made. He sees no distinction between ordinary and extraordinary political contests but only the distinction between legal and illegal whereby extraordinary politics becomes just another form of crime. Most tragically, he encourages the mystification of government power by arguing that no matter how bad the law is, any toleration of disobedience must be a worse evil. What chance is there for political improvement if the government is urged, despite the advice of history, morality, and philosophy, never to doubt the sanctity of a particular law or policy?

4. *Concerning Dissent and Civil Disobedience* (New York, 1968), p. 32.

A more recent view that this essay builds upon holds that certain acts of disobedience and refusal deserve lenient treatment and, indeed, ought not to be prosecuted where the doubts, constitutional and moral, surrounding some law or policy are so serious that no legal ruling can be considered conclusive. Speaking directly about draft resisters, Ronald Dworkin has provided an apt response to Fortas' rigid position: "The argument that because the government believes a man has committed a crime, it must prosecute him is much weaker than it seems. Society 'cannot endure' if it tolerates all disobedience; it does not follow, however, nor is there evidence, that it will collapse if it tolerates some. In the United States prosecutors have discretion whether to enforce criminal laws in particular cases. A prosecutor may properly decide not to press charges if the law breaker is young, or inexperienced, or the sole support of a family, or is repentant, or turns state's evidence, or if the law is unpopular or unworkable or generally disobeyed, or if the courts are clogged with more important cases, or for dozens of other reasons. This discretion is not license—we expect prosecutors to have good reasons for exercising it—but there are, at least *prima facie*, some good reasons for not prosecuting those who disobey draft laws out of conscience. One is the obvious reason that they act out of better motives than those who break the law out of greed or a desire to subvert the government. Another is the practical reason that our society suffers a loss if it punishes a group that includes—as the group of draft dissenters does—some of its most thoughtful and loyal citizens. Jailing such men solidifies their alienation from society, and alienates many like them who are deterred by the threat."[5] This is the modest case for extending amnesty to those who opposed the Vietnam war; it argues that, in this instance, there are "good reasons" for respecting the conscience of the disobedient citizen. Such good reasons include the questionable constitutionality of the war and the manner in which it was prosecuted, of which more shortly.

The other requirements built into Bedau's definition are intended to distinguish civil disobedience from other methods of illegal opposition. Nonviolence is essential since the purpose of

5. "On Not Prosecuting Civil Disobedience," *The New York Review of Books*, June 6, 1968, p. 14.

disobedience is to persuade others by example. Violence, whatever can be said for its tactical strengths and weaknesses, is not
an art of persuasion but a method of coercion. Thus Gandhi
used to insist that "To use brute force, to use gunpowder, is
contrary to passive resistance, for it means that we want our
opponent to do by force that which we desire but he does not.
And if such a use of force is justifiable, surely he is entitled to
do likewise by us. And so we should never come to an agreement."[6] It is the resister's desire to "come to an agreement"
that precludes his use of violence. Nonviolence is a sign of his
belief that he and the majority still share a moral code that can
harmonize their disagreement. His appeal is to that shared code.
This also explains the public character of his action; he does
not want simply to evade the law but to confront it, and thus
force others to confront the meaning of their obedience. To ac-
complish its purpose civil disobedience must be open, not
secretive.

The final criterion of civil disobedience, that it be undertaken
conscientiously, has been interpreted to demand several things.
All other methods of political or legal appeal must first be ex-
hausted. For example, civil disobedience is more defensible
when it can be shown that a person or group has been system-
atically prevented from participating in the normal political
process of, say, voting. Additionally, many would include the
demand that the lawbreaker accept the legal consequences of
his action as a further sign of his moral seriousness. The example of Socrates, who refused to obey the laws of his society
but willingly accepted punishment, is often cited as an instance
of disobedience to a law combined with fidelity to the larger social order. Taking the consequences is considered the price a
man must pay to convince others of his conscientiousness and
to encourage their identification with the beliefs that prompted
his defiance of the law.

Interpreted in this fashion, civil disobedience is most likely
where an individual or group retains some belief that the political system is open enough for a public appeal to have some
impact. The gap between the individual's convictions and the
government's actions is not yet so large that the citizen despairs
of ever closing the distance between them. But when this gap

6. M. K. Gandhi, *Non-Violent Resistance* (New York, 1961), p. 19.

is great or the punishment seems too harsh an alternative is available to the citizen, conscientious refusal.

"Conscientious refusal," according to John Rawls, "is non-compliance with a more or less direct legal injunction or administrative order."[7] Refusal to report for induction, failure to register with a draft board, and desertion were the most frequent forms that conscientious refusal took during the Vietnam war. Conscientious refusal is not a direct appeal to the public; the action is not secretive, however, since there is usually no way to avoid discovery. But while refusal may be motivated by the belief that a law is unconstitutional, the person does not look for a chance to test the law directly. Rather, refusal occurs when the law directly addresses the individual. Three factors, I believe, made such refusal more common than civil disobedience as a way of opposing the Vietnam war. First, many of the exiles were pessimistic about the chances of influencing either the government or the public through civil disobedience. Where hostility and divisions of opinion are intense, public debate—and Rawls aptly calls civil disobedience a form of public address—is simply futile. Second, many of the exiles opposed the war policy as immoral. They were not interested in testing the issue in the courts, although, as will be seen, some did resort to the courts. Finally, many of the exiles rejected the notion that one must accept the legal consequences of disobedience.

This third feature of the exiles' refusal, the unwillingness to accept punishment, evidently dismayed many persons who otherwise sympathized with that refusal. It is a point that I will want to return to in discussing the view that alternative service must be linked to amnesty, but there are several things that need to be said at once.

Three points are normally made to support the demand that the resister accept punishment. First, such submission is considered a sign of the resister's acceptance of the legal framework within which his resistance occurs. His refusal to comply with a particular law is clearly distinguished from the revolutionary's rejection of the state's authority as such. Second, it signals an absence of criminal motive; the resister informs the community that he recognizes his responsibility to be law-

7. *A Theory of Justice*, p. 368.

abiding at the same time that he announces his unwillingness to comply with this particular law. Finally, by accepting punishment the resister makes an appeal from the law to the conscience of the community, an appeal more likely to succeed when punishment is not evaded.

I have already explained why I think the American exiles chose not to make the familiar "public appeal" of civil disobedience. The other two claims for acceptance of punishment are, I believe, too sweeping and beg the question, i.e., whether or not resistance that evades punishment can be justified. If noncompliance with a particular law can be distinguished from the anarchist's rejection of all law, why equate the refusal to accept punishment for one act with a refusal to acknowledge the state's right to punish any acts? If the acceptance of punishment is being insisted upon as a demonstration of fidelity to the general system of law, are there not signs other than the acceptance of a particular punishment that indicate such fidelity? If an exile has a history of obeying all the laws of his society except the law that made him choose exile, this would seem to count as evidence of his general acceptance of the norm of obedience. As far as I know, the Vietnam war resisters were neither more nor less law-abiding than other citizens. The resister is as capable and may be as willing as any other citizen to pay his taxes, obey the laws against theft, support the civic life of his community, and in general acknowledge his legal obligations. To insist always that a political offender "pay a price" as a way of demonstrating his acceptance of the state's authority in general is to demand a price that he may reject and that we often do not need.

The closely related claim that acceptance of punishment indicates conscientiousness or sincerity is probably true, but it does not automatically follow that evasion of punishment demonstrates a lack of serious political and moral commitment. Many writers, including Abe Fortas, are mistaken in holding that no disobedience which evades punishment can be justified. By a sleight of hand that makes submission to arrest and punishment a necessary feature of justifiable civil disobedience, they then conclude that any resistance lacking this necessary feature is unjustifiable. But this begs the issue; it predetermines by strictly formal criteria what disobedience can or cannot be

morally justified.[8] Must a black who believes, perhaps with
good reason, that he cannot receive a fair trial from a white
jury accept arrest and punishment before we can even begin to
talk about the possible justification of his disobedience? What
about those persons who defied the fugitive slave law by trans-
porting southern slaves to freedom in the North by the under-
ground railroad? Is their disobedience morally unjustified because they evaded arrest and punishment? Clearly, there are
occasions where the very act of disobedience entails evasion
of punishment.

Because we are most accustomed to the resister who makes a
public appeal to the conscience of the community by submitting
to arrest and punishment, we are unaccustomed to acts of disobedience that have a more private purpose. While the exiles'
actions clearly had a public impact, they sought a private rather
than a public solution to their dilemma. They chose to go into
exile rather than to stay and fight for a change in policy or law
at home. From this perspective, accepting the legal consequences can be seen for what it is—a tactical, not a principled,
decision.

Nothing said so far relieves the resister of the responsibility
of overcoming the presumption in favor of obeying the law. To
overcome that presumption it must be shown that the state's
claim on a person's service is rightly rejected because the
method and substance of that claim violates important moral
or political principles. The case for amnesty must concentrate
on those objections to the government's policy with which
other members of the community can identify, at least to the
point that they can appreciate and consequently tolerate the
convictions that have made some men disobedients and exiles.

The War versus the Constitution

"This is really war." Thus President Lyndon Johnson announced
his decision on July 28, 1965, to send 50,000 soldiers to Vietnam.

"The Congress shall have Power to declare War . . ." (Article
I, Section 8, Clause 11, of the Constitution).

The illegality of America's military presence in Vietnam was

8. Cf. Robert T. Hall, *The Morality of Civil Disobedience* (New York, 1971), pp.
15–17.

an argument pressed by draft resisters and soldiers refusing service in Vietnam as early as 1965. The story of this legal struggle and the case against the war's constitutionality has been argued by Leon Friedman and Burt Neuborne in their book, *Unquestioning Obedience to the President*.[9] I do not want to repeat the debate over the war's constitutionality here. Rather, I want to suggest the political significance of that debate for the amnesty issue.

Doubts about the legal formality of the Vietnam war cannot be separated from the feeling among many of the exiles that the Vietnam war was "Johnson's war" or "Nixon's war." Formalism, the following of legally prescribed procedures sanctioned by custom, is what often separates might from right, "Nixon's war" from America's war. When men express confidence in the judicial system, they believe that due process is being followed; when men accept the outcome of an election even though they lose, they believe that it has been procedurally fair and open. Legitimacy and authority are created by requiring power to flow within the channels marked out by constitutional forms and the democratic ethos. Loyalty, obedience to the government, the general will for the rule of law are largely a matter of power conforming to the widely shared expectations about how power will be exercised. Conformity to these expectations becomes more, not less, critical when government policies make new and heavy demands upon citizens. Changing the condition of the country from a state of peace to a state of war is always accompanied by potential divisions of opinion. Such divisions are intensified whenever men are left with the feeling that the government's decisions are in no way their decisions. It is not a question of having one's view prevail, but the awareness that it matters that one has a view.

The requirement that Congress "declare" war is one way of increasing the probability that the concerns and interests of the public will be one of the pressures that enters into the calculations of the government. It is the only way of obtaining an unambiguous statement of the public will whereby the government's decision also becomes the public's decision. Political norms and procedures make the government responsible to the

9. (New York, 1972). Also see Alexander Bickel, "The Constitution and the War," *Commentary* 54 (July 1972):49–55.

governed and increase the probability that the governed will support the government. The general will for the rule of law is not the product of a decision here and there but of the widespread belief that decisions are being made according to customary and constitutional patterns. Looking at the pattern by which the government made the war policy in Vietnam highlights the extent to which new and demanding policies departed from democratic expectations. Consistent administration understatements about the nature and costs of American involvement in Vietnam, the proclamation of major policy decisions by the president without any public knowledge of the multiplying consequences of those decisions, and the passage of congressional resolutions that resolved nothing—these were the techniques substituted for the formal constitutional procedures for committing the country to war.

Widespread resistance to the war was practically guaranteed by the methods used to commit the country to war. In such circumstances, the price of law enforcement becomes too high—increased antagonism between the government and its critics and, finally, between citizen and citizen, antagonisms that require unity to be held together by force rather than by a sense of shared interests. Far from being a threat to the basic order of American democracy, the acts of the exiles opened up a needed public debate on how far the government had wandered from the basic constitutional order. This debate is far from ended, but it is wise to agree with Dworkin that "When the law is uncertain, in the sense that a plausible case can be made on both sides, then a citizen who follows his own judgment is not behaving unfairly. Our practices permit and encourage him to follow his own judgment in such cases. For that reason, our government has a special responsibility to try to protect him, and soften his predicament, whenever it can do so without great damage to other policies . . . the path of fairness lies in tolerance."[10]

The way back to democratic acceptance of the rule of law begins with the recognition of the suspicions surrounding the war's origins and the integrity of those whose actions served as a catalyst for those suspicions. An amnesty for those who refused to submit to a policy that they were never given the op-

10. Page 14.

portunity to make *their* policy should, if nonpunitive, restore in some small measure the exiles' and, equally important, our confidence in American democracy. Amnesty can smooth out not only the plight of the exiles but the plight of the American political community.

POWER VERSUS DECENCY

American involvement in the Vietnam war produced more profound moral discourse about the terms upon which this country goes to war and its methods of warfare than perhaps any other war in its history. It is fairly easy to account for this. There was, first, never a clear decision to go to war. Involvement in Vietnam was drawn out over a large number of years, and each step was attended by increasing criticism. Also, the government invented a whole new vocabulary, for describing the war, that was so corrupt or, at best, so deceptive that the citizen had to labor at deciphering just what the government's actions amounted to. American troops entering Laos became "checkers"; bombing was "protective reaction"; refugee camps were "pacification centers"; indiscriminate shooting was a "free-fire zone"; and a sunk sampan became a "waterborne logistic craft." The spiraling nature of the war was accompanied by spiraling statements about American objectives. Aid to a friendly power became a struggle against North Vietnamese and then Chinese "aggression." The high point of the war was a contest for democracy (a notion that always was a mockery· and is now mocked by President Thieu). Was the Vietnam war, the American citizen might well wonder, a war of national liberation, a revolutionary movement, a communist movement, a civil war, a war pitting China and/or the Soviet Union against the United States? The clash of responses to the war—support and opposition, service and exile—reflected the clash of ideas about the war.

Whatever might be said about the Vietnam war, the United States was not under direct attack from an outside aggressor. Any American national interest in South Vietnam had to be inferred from some interpretation of the Vietnamese political situation. But there was no agreement about which interpretation was most adequate, and this created the roots of resistance to government policy. The most consistent interpretation offered by American governments argued that Vietnam was a "testing ground." Communist success in Vietnam, it was argued, would encourage further acts of aggression elsewhere. Every judgment in this rationale for our massive commitment in Vietnam is open to serious debate. Critics[11] have made five particular points.

In a large part of the world, where nation-building is still taking place, revolutionary conditions exist that it is impossible to completely suppress. Any revolutionary movement today is likely to have an element of communist ideology. If the United States always takes a stand against communism, it will constantly be on the side of the status quo. But the status quo in many of these countries is usually contrary to the ideals that America traditionally encouraged, e.g., reduction of economic inequalities and the overthrow of politically repressive governments.

America's Vietnam policy assumed that communism is a monolithic force and that communist insurrections are somehow orchestrated by China or the Soviet Union. But it is not clear that a communist "victory" in South Vietnam would in fact enlarge the power of Russia and/or China. Such a victory might simply contribute to the balkanization or pluralism of communism. Indeed, if communist movements do not act in concert, it is in the United States' interest to encourage this balkanization. Yet American intervention in South Vietnam made the Vietnamese revolutionary movement more rather than less dependent upon China.

It is only a guess that an American "victory" in South Vietnam would have discouraged revolutionary outbreaks in other

11. Cf. Quentin L. Quade, "The United States and Wars of National Liberation," in Richard A. Falk, ed., The Vietnam War and International Law (Princeton, 1968), 1:102–26. On American just war doctrine, see Robert Tucker, The Just War (Baltimore, 1960). A more philosophical inquiry into the differences between just and unjust methods of warfare is undertaken by Thomas Nagel, "War and Massacre," Philosophy and Public Affairs 1 (Winter 1972):123–44. On the questionable legality of American methods of warfare in Vietnam and the issue of war crimes, see Erwin Knoll and Judith Nies McFadden, eds., War Crimes and the American Conscience (New York, 1970). The direction that Congress might go in recapturing some role in the making of war policy is suggested by the hearings before the Senate Foreign Relations Committee, War Powers Legislation, 92d Cong., 1st sess., 1971.

countries. Even if it deterred developments comparable to Vietnam in some countries, how many such outbreaks could the United States successfully become engaged in without further damage to itself?

Given the difficulties of fighting a guerrilla war, could the United States have achieved its limited political objective of a stable Saigon government without using military tactics that violated many of the other values Americans profess? Was the American government willing to purchase such an objective even at the cost of agreeing with the American officer who stated that "It was necessary to destroy the village in order to save it"? This was a policy that equated desolation with peace.

The argument that America had to stick it out in Vietnam so as not to lose credibility with its other allies was particularly disingenuous. No major Western European country traditionally allied with the United States gave full support to our effort in Vietnam. Indeed, many of these countries became critical of the United States because of Vietnam.

Men who shared these particular criticisms of America's errand in Vietnam, whether they were draft evaders or deserters, acted responsibly in refusing to serve. It is never easy to break attachments to family, friends, and nation. Even for those exiles who successfully adjusted to their new lives in a strange country, it is not easy to accept the fact that "you can never go home again." Writing in a Canadian newspaper a young deserter described this feeling:

> The question is always asked in innocence, always framed in a voice of concern, always with a gently painful naivete. Every Canadian I've met gets around to it sooner or later. "You can never go back, can you?" they ask. . . . The question pulls out images topsy-turvy, a mixed bag of memories good and bad: flashes of a tiny Nebraska town tucked away in the western badlands, of early years yearning for the uniform of an American soldier, of an Air Force Academy appointment declined, of fruitless protest marches and finally the induction notice and the brief fling with the compromise in the U.S. Army. And underneath, the persistent refrain: "You can't go home again. . . ."
>
> Home—the U.S.—is a jangled chaos, a great nation writhing in contradictions, groping for a solution through force or

flowers. But it's still home, still a magnet whose force field cannot be ignored, even by the thousands of young men like myself who have chosen to reject it rather than participate in what we consider its greatest folly. . . . [There] is a fear that most of us will carry into middle age, a fear born of being wanted for a crime we do not consider a crime. We will carry this, and the desire to go home just once, and the labels "draft dodger" and "deserter" and we will always answer the innocent question: "you can never go home, can you? . . ." History may judge us as cowards or heroes, but we are simply young men caught in a vortex of events whirling beyond our control. We had a choice— war, prison or exile—we made it, and we will make the best of it.[12]

Unless one naïvely assumes that the world is the best of all possible worlds or despairingly believes that everything in the world is a necessary evil, there will always be occasion for actions aimed at closing the distance between what power decrees and justice demands. Awareness of the tension between power and morality concludes this part of the case for amnesty. Namely, we should demand that men respond to their sense of decency rather than power whenever their principles and convictions are ideals that we can sympathize with and thus tolerate. *When men behave as we think that citizens like them ought to behave, it is not fitting to punish their actions.*[13]

BEYOND LAW AND PUNISHMENT

The rule of law has come to stand for many things. In international relations it means the replacement of force by legal methods as a way of settling disputes. At other times, it sum-

---

12. Cited in Williams, *The New Exiles*, pp. 327-28.
13. This is the central argument of Ronald Dworkin's essay "On Not Prosecuting Civil Disobedience." Dworkin ties his case for setting aside prosecution to the belief implicit in any act of civil disobedience that the challenged law is not valid law, that is, constitutional. My argument goes somewhat beyond this position, that *in the case of the exiles* punishment should also be set aside for disobedience to a policy of doubtful morality. Perhaps it should also be added that both Dworkin's thesis and the brief for amnesty depend upon the conclusion that punishment would serve no practical purpose and would negate other worthwhile values. This, of course, was the argument of the preceding chapter.

marizes the basic rights of citizens guaranteed by a written or
an unwritten constitution. Directed at officials, the rule of law
commands them to govern according to fixed rules rather than
by personal will. Addressed to the citizen, it reminds him that
the law must be obeyed and that no man is to be judge in his
own case.

Common to all of these meanings is an agreement to be rule-
following. What the legalist and many others are apt to forget
is that that agreement is a precondition of the rule of law, not
something created by it. Without such agreement the law is a
"homeless ghost."[14] What lies beyond the law are those conditions within which the agreement to be rule-following is
forged. The stability and worth of democratic government demands something more than the state's power to punish. There
must exist a tacit agreement, what de Tocqueville called a *consensus universalis*, to abide by the social compact that creates
a government of laws, not men. This social compact includes
more than majority rule or electoral politics, features of the
democratic rule of law. The success of the contract depends
upon a widespread belief that the benefits of membership in the
political community outweigh the burdens. The core of this belief is the feeling of reciprocity—the confidence that, as regards
our rights and duties, good faith is being kept with us.

Obedience to government and acceptance of the prevailing
notion of rule of law are as much products of habit as anything
else. Time tends to wrap any state in the cloth of legitimacy.
But at two points in the life of any state, habit is not sufficient—
at the birth of a state and when the state begins to make on its
citizens new demands which depart from the expectations embedded in its political traditions.[15] The thesis here is that
American policy in Vietnam represented a departure from
American political traditions about how rulers will exercise
their power and that that policy imposed new burdens without
a satisfactory corresponding account of the benefits.

Amnesty has as much, indeed more, to do with the nature of
American society and the terms upon which political authority
will be renegotiated as it does with the fate of the exiles. Am-

14. M. R. Cohen, *Reason and Law* (Glencoe, Ill., 1950), p. 80.
15. Cf. John H. Schaar, "Legitimacy in the Modern State," in Philip Green
and Sanford Levinson, eds., *Power and Community* (New York, 1970), p. 287.

nesty is one of the possible terms that can become part of the new social contract. I see no evidence for either the warning that the American social fabric could not mend without the exiles or the fear that amnesty would irreparably embitter some. The point is simply that a country is one type of society when it grants amnesty and another type when it does not.

Those who worry about the sincerity of political offenders or fear that shirkers can escape under an amnesty proclamation divert attention from the substantive historical and political conditions that give rise to a war resistance movement. The trouble with most civil disobedience theory is that it encourages precisely this sort of speculation. The assumption is that one is dealing with an individual who has perhaps conscientiously defied the state's law. To deal with this problem, we are told to evaluate his conscientiousness and then to decide what cost, if any, he should pay for his disobedience. But this is a misstatement of what happened in America during the Vietnam war. No one has seen this more clearly than Hannah Arendt: "The greatest fallacy in the present debate seems to me that assumption that we are dealing with individuals, who pit themselves subjectively and conscientiously against the laws and customs of the community—an assumption that is shared by the defenders and detractors of civil disobedience. The fact is that we are dealing with organized minorities, who stand against assumed and nonvocal, though hardly 'silent,' majorities, and I think it is undeniable that these majorities have changed in mood and opinion to an astounding degree under the pressure of the minorities. It has been the misfortune of recent debates that they have been dominated largely by jurists—lawyers, judges, and other men of law—for they must find it difficult to recognize the civil disobedient as a member of a group rather than to see him as an individual lawbreaker, and hence a potential defendant in court."[16] Just as determining individual blame or innocence was obviously irrelevant to the reconciliation of the North and South after the Civil War, so the problem at the end of the Vietnam war was not mainly one of individual blame but a matter of renegotiating the political good so that it could as far as possible become a common good. When a large segment of the population dissents, through draft evasion,

16. "Civil Disobedience," pp. 98-99.

desertion, or illegal protest, the courtroom or review board is the wrong place for rediscovering that democratic pluralism which makes room for diversity within unity, dissent within consent.

To be more specific, the demand for alternative service or for exiles to "earn their way home" as a condition of amnesty looks mainly to the past in search of individual guilt or innocence when what is needed is an accommodation that makes room for a whole group of dissenting citizens. The demand for a penalty undermines all of the major values that make amnesty a worthy experiment.[17] Amnesty means something more than setting aside prosecution and punishment; it means forgoing recriminations and denunciations. Amnesty is an assertion that the divisions over the Vietnam war were so deeply rooted that assigning guilt or innocence to draft evaders or deserters was never the main problem. Amnesty does not foreclose continued controversy about either the wisdom or the folly of the Vietnam war or the responsibilities of those in and out of government, but it recognizes that the controversy has two sides. Peter Steinfels describes the risks with which both government and citizens are confronted by the issue of amnesty: "In one case, amnesty implies a recognition of a certain justice in the cause of those being amnestied. In another case, it implies no such thing, but rather reflects the power and virtue of those *granting* the amnesty. In short, the whole thing is pretty ambiguous, and many zealous people on the left, perhaps some of the war resisters themselves, can make as good a case against amnesty from *their* perspective as can the conservatives on the right. Amnesty will render certain benefits to both parties in the current profound dispute among American citizens; in the same way it requires certain concessions from both parties. . . . Some

17. It is clear that the advocates of alternative service or "earned re-entry" consider such service as punitive. Thus, Senator Taft, in introducing his conditional amnesty bill in the Senate, approvingly quoted the sentiments of one of his constituents who had written: "It is my contention that many of these young men could be induced or persuaded to return to their native land to assume their responsibilities and become useful citizens again. I do not mean grant them amnesty, but they must earn their return and regain their normal heritage and birthright through hard work and proof that they are honest, sincere, and thankful to be re-accepted by the land of their birth": *Congressional Record*, 92d Cong., 1st sess., December 14, 1971. I suspect that men ready to admit everything this statement demands would never have become exiles in the first place.

would argue against amnesty on the basis that it would involve a kind of national confession of guilt on the question of the war. . . . On the other hand, amnesty also involves a certain recognition by the people being granted amnesty of the unity of our society and the ties that bind them to it. Accepting amnesty does imply, on their part, a nebulous willingness to get on with business *within* our society, even if that business is only to continue their debate over American foreign policy."[18] Amnesty involves risks on both sides; but these risks are worth taking so as to return to the exiles the freedom of living or traveling in America and to reaffirm public acceptance of the democratic ideal of limited loyalty to a limited state.

Conclusions

A universal and unconditional amnesty should be granted, by Congress or the president, to all of those who felt that their first duty was to stop contributing to the disfigurement of the world in Vietnam. Among those who merit amnesty are persons who refused to serve in the military in support of the Vietnam war, whether they are in prison or in exile; soldiers who refused either to go to Vietnam or, as in the case of Dr. Levy, to train others for service in Vietnam; soldiers who deserted because of their aversion to the war, and soldiers who received a less than honorable discharge because of their opposition to the war; civilians who took part in nonviolent protests against the war, including the destroying of draft files and counseling draft resistance. Some would distinguish among these groups, granting amnesty, for example, to draft resisters but not to deserters. This is the case with both of the amnesty bills first introduced in Congress—one sponsored by Representative Edward I. Koch, a Democrat, and the other sponsored by Senator Robert Taft, Jr., a Republican. The main reason offered for discriminating between resisters and deserters is the contention that soldiers have a special obligation since they take an oath of service. But any oath or promise is qualified by subsequent circumstances. A soldier who refuses patently illegal or immoral commands is not thought to have broken his prom-

18. In Polner, *When Can I Come Home?*, pp. 124–25.

ise. Conscientious desertion differs from such a case in that there is argument and counterargument about the legality or morality of the demanded service. But it is the existence of this controversy and the resister's dilemma in choosing between competing promises or loyalties that amnesty is intended to acknowledge. A deserter may act out of the same motives of opposition to a war as someone who evades the draft. The major difference between them is the circumstances in which they find themselves at the moment their abhorrence of a war occurs. Both are confronted with the same problem: whether to submit to the law and defy their consciences or affirm their consciences and defy the law. The timing and circumstances surrounding that problem do not change its basic character. An amnesty that excludes some from its benefits is arbitrary, setting aside the punishment for some but not for others sharing the same convictions. And while statistics are difficult to find, some impressions do emerge from the reports of those who visited the American exile communities in Canada, France, and Sweden. Deserters were more likely than draft resisters to come from the lower economic and blue-collar groups. They were less likely to be college educated; many reported that they were unfamiliar with ways to avoid the draft. In short, an amnesty that excludes deserters penalizes them both for the timing of their resistance and their lesser political sophistication. What happens to political offenders should not be determined by the chance of timing or the accident of education.

Although conscientious refusal to serve in a war appears primarily as negative, since it is a denial of a duty expected by the state, it may also be an affirmation of that which is valuable in every man and essential to democracy—conscientious citizenship. War resisters' actions may be a positive force in other ways. During the Vietnam war, the exiles reminded us how far American governments had departed from constitutional ideals and the democratic ethos in committing America to war without an open public debate. The American exiles affirmed that life is too valuable to be spent for, at best, marginal national interests, as was the case in the Vietnamese war. Such men are not very far from Albert Camus' rebel, about whom Camus wrote, "The logic of the rebel is to want to serve justice so as not to add to the injustice of the human condition, to insist on plain language so as not to increase the universal falsehood, and to wager, in spite of human misery, for happiness."[19]

The American exiles never needed our forgiveness nor should we forget the tensions between power and decency represented by their actions. Amnesty is a way of returning to society men who, when we look closer, are friends rather than enemies of the democratic community.

19. *The Rebel* (New York, 1956), p. 285.

UNIVERSITY OF FLORIDA MONOGRAPHS

Social Sciences